Published by Familius LLC, www.familius.com

Familius books are available at special discounts for bulk purchases for sales promotions, family or corporate use. Special editions, including personalized covers, excerpts of existing books, or books with corporate logos, can be created in large quantities for special needs. For more information, contact Premium Sales at 559-876-2170 or email specialmarkets@familius.com.

Library of Congress Catalog-in-Publication Data
2015952076
ISBN 9781942934066

Cover and book design by David Miles
Edited by Lindsay Sandberg
Photography credit: Shutterstock.com

10 9 8 7 6 5 4 3 2 1

First Edition

Printed in China

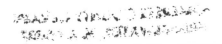

THE
STEVIA
SOLUTION
COOKBOOK

SATISFY YOUR SWEET TOOTH WITH THE
NO-CALORIES, NO-CARB, NO-CHEMICAL,
ALL-NATURAL, HEALTHY SWEETENER

CALEB WARNOCK

FAMILIUS

CONTENTS

AUTHOR'S NOTE

THE "BITTER" TRUTH ABOUT STEVIA AND THE SOLUTION

There has always been one problem with stevia in the United States—everyone who lauds its sweet power tends to overlook the not-so-sweet difficulties of using stevia. Many, many people have tried stevia and given up on it for one simple reason: stevia doesn't taste *exactly* like white sugar, nor does it work like sugar in recipes. Trying to replace sugar totally with stevia is where stevia users fail.

For a long time, I, too, wanted to be able to replace all the sugar in my diet with stevia. But that was too austere to be sustainable. The truth is when we make stevia "all or nothing," we are missing the whole point.

We like sugar.

Okay, let's be honest. We *love* sugar. We love the way it tastes. It is hard to find anyone who doesn't consume some form of sugar for three meals each day.

No one should be surprised that when asked to give up sugar completely for stevia, the world has collectively said, "No, thanks."

But we *can* use stevia to cut out huge amounts of sugar from our food without ever noticing the difference. I am convinced that this is the power of stevia to save our health.

I call this book *The Stevia Solution* because it all comes down to ratios. Our family has been able to cut at least two-thirds of the sugar from our lives using stevia, and we've given up nothing in terms of flavor. When we use stevia-and-fruit puree to replace half of the sugar—or more—from a recipe, we are making big progress.

Imagine what would happen if we each gave up half the sugar we eat. We would be far healthier. We would be able to slow, or perhaps even halt, the march of type 2 diabetes, along with what scientists are now calling "type 3 diabetes": dementia.

And one more thing: The search for a healthier sweetener has never been more in vogue than it is today. There is a slew of so-called "healthy natural sweeteners" out there aiming to replace refined sugar in our diets. These include agave, monk fruit extract, coconut sugar, brown rice syrup, molasses, honey, and maple syrup. But all of these have at least two glaring problems that are almost never discussed: their effect on the glycemic index is pretty much exactly the same as that of refined white sugar—whether that sugar comes from sugar beets or sugar cane—and the alternatives are often less sweet than sugar and contain more calories ounce per ounce!

In this book, I will refer frequently to the *glycemic index*. The glycemic index is a measure of how foods affect our blood sugar. Simple sugars and starches (white flour, white rice, etc.) all spike the glycemic index. I will also refer to the *glycemic load*, which is an estimate of how much a food will raise a person's glucose level after eating it. A food with a high glycemic index or glycemic load puts increased stress on our bodies as it tries to stabilize blood sugar levels. The quick rise and fall of sugar levels in the blood is what causes chronic low-grade inflammation in our tissues and leads to type 2 diabetes and perhaps type 3 diabetes (dementia). No matter how healthy your agave syrup or honey is, it spikes your blood sugar exactly like refined sugar, causing exactly the same long-term health and weight issues.

Not stevia, though.

So why hasn't stevia replaced traditional sugar yet?

Several reasons. First, makers of artificial sweeteners fought against FDA approval of stevia for decades. The FDA finally approved stevia for use as a sweetener in the United States in 2008, following years of battles between big corporations and health interests. For decades before official approval was finally granted, a small and quiet grassroots movement centered on stevia had been building in the United States, led by families looking to protect their own health and that of their children without giving up the sweet foods that give life pleasure and joy. Companies had tried to import stevia only to have the government seize it. Stevia lovers had tried to introduce stevia to the nation with recipes and desserts only to find themselves afoul of the FDA. Thankfully, today the government has finally given stevia and stevia extracts the green light, causing a boom in use of this natural plant sweetener.

There are huge benefits to stevia, but to make stevia work best for your family, it helps to understand how stevia and traditional white processed sugar are different:

- **STEVIA HAS NO BULK.** A teaspoon of stevia can replace roughly a cup of sugar. Because the amounts just don't match up, this makes it difficult to substitute stevia in recipes that call for sugar.

- **STEVIA DOESN'T BROWN.** Sugar melts and caramelizes, which can give foods and desserts important tastes and textures that you simply can't get from stevia.

- **STEVIA IS A "BACK OF THE TONGUE" FLAVOR.** Processed white sugar from the grocery store is immediately sweet on the tongue. But human taste buds register the sweetness of stevia differently than processed sugar, causing about a two-second delay before sweetness registers with the brain. This causes problems because it allows the tongue to pick up other flavors first; the tastes of flour, mint, butter, and peanut butter, for example, are all registered by the tongue before the sweetness of stevia.

- **STEVIA HAS A SLIGHTLY BITTER AFTERTASTE.** But there is a solution. Because stevia is extraordinarily sweet, it can only be used in tiny amounts. This makes it difficult to convert favorite recipes. Traditional sugar has a large window of flavor forgiveness; if you put in a little more than the recipe calls for, it's okay. If you put in a little less than the recipe calls for, the flavor is still good. Stevia, on the other hand, has a much smaller flavor forgiveness window. If you use too little, you will taste no sweetness at all. If you use even a bit too much, the flavor will be bitter. The solution to these problems is to use stevia in combination with other natural ingredients.

I spent three years creating the recipes in this book, originally for my own health. I made thousands of cakes, pies, cookies, and more, tweaking and perfecting these recipes, which are authentically healthy with no gimmicks yet truly sweet and delicious without that "diet food" flavor.

Healthy, delicious food is important to me. I want to improve my health without changing my lifestyle or depriving my sweet tooth. And, now, I can honestly say that my family has found the solution: the Stevia Solution.

STEVIA
101

The stevia plant closely resembles spearmint, peppermint, and lemon balm.

STEVIA: THE ALL-NATURAL HONEY LEAF

Stevia is a leafy green herb with sugary leaves. Most people don't believe it until they taste it. For centuries, the Guaraní tribes of Paraguay have grown and loved these candy-flavored leaves, benefiting daily from the natural health stevia provides. They call it *Khaa Jee*, which means "honey leaf." Stevia is the world's only all-natural, calorie-free, nonglycemic, herbal sweetener.

At our family's home in the Rocky Mountains, we have grown stevia in our backyard gardens and greenhouse for years, using it in our kitchen as a healthy sugar alternative.

Because I have authored nine books on gardening and self-reliant living, thousands of people have toured our backyard gardens. They *ooh* and *ahh* at the sunchokes, my collection of antique and rare medicinal herbs, my historic lettuces, the world's rarest onions, and my pineapple-flavored white strawberries. They examine unheard-of varieties of antique beans, perennial wheat, albino beets, and gold raspberries. They walk right past the stevia without pausing, without noticing it, without seeing it as something remarkable, even life altering.

All of that changes when I let them taste it.

"What is it?" they ask as I hand them a leaf.

"Just trust me," I say. "You've never tasted anything like this in your life. Tear off a tiny piece and put it on your tongue."

They don't know what to expect. I never get tired of watching their surprise. They slowly, sometimes suspiciously, put the leaf on their tongue, and their confusion melts away as they taste its strong candy-like sweetness. A wide smile brightens their faces, every single time.

"This is stevia," I say. "The world's best sugar."

The health benefits of stevia are remarkable.

STEVIA IS 100 PERCENT NATURAL

Wild stevia plants still grow in the subtropical regions of Paraguay, drinking in the warmth, humidity, and abundant rains and blooming with a new crop of sugar-flavored leaves each year. The plant is all-natural—not hybrid, not genetically modified. The leaves can be used fresh or dried. The sugary flavor can be extracted from the leaves at home, and commercial stevia extracts are finally widely available.

"There can have been few botanical discoveries quite so dramatic as the realization that the leaves of *Stevia rebaudiana . . .* are so highly sweet," writes A. Douglas Kinghorn in a scientific monograph of the plant.[1]

From a botanical point of view, stevia is an outlier. There are more than 230 species in the stevia genus, but only *Stevia rebaudiana* has the sought-after sugary leaves. The candy-like flavor comes because the plant has the unusual and rare ability to accumulate large numbers of metabolites in its leaves. As stevia metabolizes food and sunlight, eight different sweet-tasting metabolites occur naturally in its leaves. Kinghorn says stevia is "certainly very unusual" because few other plants in the world collect such a high number of metabolites in their leaves; stevia has more than 150 total. That eight of them are strongly sugary is Mother Nature's gift to food and health lovers everywhere.

This wonder of the botanical world has become a wonder for anyone today looking to have their sugary cake and keep their health, too.

1. A. Douglas Kinghorn, ed., *Stevia: The Genus Stevia* (New York: Taylor & Francis, 2002).

31 REASONS TO LOVE THIS COOKBOOK (AND A FREE GIFT)

T his cookbook has a larger purpose than offering a few recipes with less sugar—it is supposed to help you adjust your diet without truly changing your lifestyle. It is also supposed to give you the reasons why you can and should take the challenge of bettering your health. So there are many reasons to love this cookbook.

1. **A FREE GIFT.** Everyone loves a free gift, so let's start this list with that. I am so passionate about stevia that I am offering a free sample of either pure powdered stevia leaf or pure powdered stevia extract, 90 percent strength (the real stuff), to anyone who buys this book. To redeem your gift, click the "Free Offers" tab at SeedRenaissance.com.

2. **AT LAST, STEVIA USED RIGHT!** When used with precision, and in combination with other natural foods, stevia is a perfect sweetener with no calories, no glycemic impact, no inflammation, and, ultimately, no guilt.

3. **AN HONEST EXPLANATION OF STEVIA'S STRENGTHS AND WEAKNESSES AS WELL AS SOLUTIONS.** Stevia must be used correctly to taste right, and that means using it in combination with other natural foods. It is not enough to do what others have done and ignore the bitterness that can be associated with stevia or the confusing array of the "percent strength" of stevia on store shelves. I have worked to tell the truth about stevia and to create solutions for making stevia useful to every family.

4. **NO "DIET FOOD."** The whole goal of this cookbook is to make the desserts you love healthy without that "diet food" flavor that must be endured but is never loved.

5. **REAL FOODS IN EVERY RECIPE.** I use natural, real ingredients to increase the protein, flatten the glycemic load, and reduce or replace the sugars and fats in your favorite desserts without removing the flavor. The foundation of each of the recipes in this book is a pineapple-pear puree that makes it possible to remove the bitter flavor from stevia. Adding whole, real fruit to brownies, for example, might sound off-putting, but you'll never even know it's there—and neither will your kids or grandkids.

6. **THE TRUTH ABOUT SUGAR DANGERS.** You've experienced enough Internet rumors pawning fake information in an attempt to make money on your desire to be

healthier. In this book, you will find concrete, easy-to-understand information and the latest research about the real dangers of sugar and how it affects your health and your kids' health, too.

7. **ADDED PROTEIN FOR NUTRITION.** Can dessert be real food instead of just a sugar high? The answer, found in the pages of this cookbook, is a resounding *Yes!* Protein is the building block of a healthy, energetic body. Even the Sweet & Healthy Powdered Sugar Substitute recipe in this book is protein rich—but you won't taste it.

8. **A LONGER LIFE.** The diseases that are most likely to affect our health and the health of our children and grandchildren are obesity and type 2 diabetes. This cookbook takes a big step toward getting rid of the sugar-related diseases that plague us.

9. **FAST AND SIMPLE RECIPES.** Many of the desserts in this cookbook are quick and easy to make. Even the sugar cookies take less than 15 minutes to make—start to finish! I honestly believe that simplicity is the spice of life. Can you make the world's healthiest powdered sugar substitute at home in less than 90 seconds? You can with this cookbook! I have tried to keep most of the recipes in this cookbook simple, because no one has time for elaborate productions in the kitchen. These recipes are real food for real people.

10. **THE HOMEMADE RENAISSANCE.** Cooking at home has been a dying art for two decades, with fewer and fewer people bothering to cook from scratch. Julia Child inspired us, but most of us now turn to prepared foods from chain stores and restaurants, frozen food, and plain quick food. Cakes are made from boxed mixes, if they come out of our kitchen ovens at all; more often they come ready made from the store. This cookbook makes it easy to craft quick, simple, healthy, and (most importantly) mouthwatering treats from scratch.

11. **"OUR BIGGEST PROBLEM."** Someone told me that the biggest problem with obesity in America is portion control. I have not forgotten that view in this book, though it may seem as though I have. Every recipe in this book is purposefully sized. There are no cakes the size of small islands, no batches of cookies to feed a legion. The recipes can be doubled if needed, but I have kept the portions small.

12. **NO FADS, NO TRENDS.** It seems like every celebrity on the planet suddenly becomes a health guru with a miracle product to endorse. But there are no for-profit pseudomiracles in this book, no fly-by-night fads. There is no miracle product in this book—just natural, healthy recipes made with stevia, fruit, and a few other natural-health superstars.

13. **NO DIETS.** I have seen many people go on dramatic diets, lose a bunch of weight, and then crash because they weren't getting the nutrients that they needed. Then they regained all the weight that they had lost—plus a little more. We can do better. Say no to diets. Purposeful, meaningful, joyful eating is where health is found. Above all, I want this cookbook to be useful to the health, happiness, and taste buds of you and your family.

14. **NO SUGAR CELIBACY.** Speaking of diets, let me confess something: I used to be obese and massively unhappy. One day, I decided to become a sugar celibate. I decided to never eat sugar again. When I met my wife, I had not eaten sugar in nearly three years. She thought that was the stupidest thing she had ever heard and told me to stop being stupid. When I started developing these recipes, I never thought they would become a cookbook; I was just making the recipes for myself and my family so that we could be healthy without giving up the sweet life. As this cookbook proves, it is possible to be healthy without being a sugar celibate. That's enough to make me smile.

15. **BELOVED, CLASSIC RECIPES.** Believe it or not, one of the hardest recipes in this book was the brownie recipe. Everyone loves brownies. It took me three years and hundreds of failed recipes before I created the brownie and chocolate frosting recipes in this book. For three years, my family turned up their noses at every single variation of a healthy brownie that I produced. I almost gave up. But now I have a no-guilt brownie recipe that my family will eat along with a host of other classics, including chocolate chip cookies, chocolate cake, and sugar cookies.

16. **NEW CLASSICS.** My very favorite recipe in this book is one that I believe is new to the world—Valentine Pie. This recipe grew out of my love for raspberries and pie. I have never seen recipes for Mulled Christmas Lemonade, Perfect Sugar-Free Jam, and Barcelo Watermelon Punch anywhere before, and I think they will stand the test of time and become new classics.

17. **REAL SOLUTIONS FROM A REAL FAMILY.** We have kids and grandkids at our house, and we are passionate about protecting their health. I created the chocolate chip cookie, hot chocolate, and frosting recipes with them in mind. They want treats. And, hey, I want treats too! I want to be able to give them hot chocolate after sledding in the winter without the guilt of sugar. The little kids love to cook with me in the kitchen; they all love to make chocolate chip cookies with me, break-ing the eggs, pouring the vanilla, stirring the dough. We always eat half the raw dough. Always. These are not family moments I want to give up, but I am also responsible for protecting their health. These kids mean everything to me, and

at the end of my life, I want to know that we raised them to be healthy, happy, useful members of society. This book—every recipe—is for them.

18. **HOMEMADE FLAVORS.** I grew up in a tiny rural town of ninety people where everyone knew everyone. We had to bring people in from all the little surrounding towns just to have enough people to fill the church. Once a year, there was a church fundraising bazaar with a cakewalk; it was one of the highlights of my childhood. Winning one of those home-baked, made-from-scratch cakes is something now lost to the world—no one cooks like that anymore. I think the recipes in this stevia cookbook capture both that nostalgic feeling and the love that the women of my childhood put into those cakes.

19. **WHY IS THIS RECIPE HEALTHY?** One thing that was important to me in this book was giving clear, concrete, factual explanations for each recipe, explaining why they are healthy yet tasty.

20. **REAL JAM.** Since word has spread that I was working on this book, the number-one-most-requested recipe was stevia jam, which you will find in these pages. Both the jam and pastry gel recipes focus on preserving the authentic flavors of fresh fruit. One of my pet peeves is jams and jellies that cloy the tongue, vaporizing the flavor of the fruit behind a blast of sugar. Yuck. I savor backyard, sun-kissed fruit flavors, and I hope you will agree that my jam and pastry gel recipes accomplish that goal.

21. **TIPS AND TRICKS.** Some things are only learned the hard way—like knowing to bake sugar cookies for exactly six minutes, when to use a hand mixer and when to use a whisk, and when to leave delicate cookies to cool on the baking sheet instead of removing them. When I recommend using the lowest heat possible for a recipe in this cookbook, it comes from hard-won experience. I hope my directions—created after months of mistakes—will make your baking simple and easy!

22. **DEFINITIONS OF BASIC TERMS.** One surprise over the past few years, since my first *Forgotten Skills of Self-Sufficiency* book became a popular seller, is how many people tell me they want to learn basic skills because they were never taught them growing up. I grew up with parents and grandparents who baked and cooked, so knowing the difference between a soft boil and a rolling boil comes more easily to me. In this book, I have tried to teach all the basics you will need for baking success. Then you can pass on your skills to your kids and grandkids, making them masters in the scratch-cook kitchen.

23. **RECIPES FOR EVERY OCCASION.** Within these pages, you will find my recipes for green smoothies, medicinal smoothies, savory barbecue sauce, and pizza sauce. And holiday recipes, too. I love holidays, especially the food. In this book, you will find recipes for Christmas, Valentine's Day, birthdays, special occasions, Thanksgiving, and everyday desserts too.

24. **DESSERTS FOR THE "HAVES."** When I thought about what I wanted to accomplish with these recipes, one thing I felt strongly about was creating recipes that would satisfy both the "haves" and the "have nots"—by which I mean those who have health and those who don't. Those who "have" health sometimes fall victim to the false belief that their health is ironclad, that they can eat anything they want. Sadly, not just the morbidly obese develop type 2 diabetes and its myriad, painful, expensive complications—20 percent of those who develop type 2 diabetes are at a healthy weight. I wanted to create a cookbook filled with desserts that you could take to a party and never mention that they are healthy and the plate would be empty at the end of the night. I wanted to create desserts that people who have health would crave, whether or not they knew these recipes were healthy.

25. **DESSERTS FOR THE "HAVE NOTS."** At the same time, I wanted desserts that were healthy for most everyone. I'm not diabetic, so I'm not an expert at determining whether every recipe in this book is safe for diabetics, but I can say with confidence that the desserts in this cookbook are far healthier than traditional desserts. It was my goal to create great flavor that would do no harm to our children and grandchildren while being enjoyable to the world.

26. **FOODS THAT HELP FIGHT INFLAMMATION.** As explained earlier in this book, one of the most serious long-term consequences of eating too much sugar is chronic low-grade inflammation, which can irreversibly damage the tissues of the body. Inflammation causes pain, flattens the immune system, and makes it harder and harder to resist sickness and maintain health. The recipes in this book have low amounts of sugar or none at all without sacrificing flavor. Don't take my word for it; try them yourself!

27. **PREBIOTIC IS PROBIOTIC.** Probiotics are good living bacteria and fungi that are absolutely essential for correct digestion. If you want a happy stomach and a healthy gut, you must have probiotics—the good bacteria and fungi living in you. They must colonize in fiber if you are to have true health, and they can only do that when you eat a regular diet of fiber. So when you are eating your dessert, just remember that you are making a happy prebiotic home from the probiotics that will bring you health. Not bad for a dessert cookbook, right?

28. **SATIATING FOOD.** Fake food rushes through our body. Real food—food with protein and fiber—moves slower, making us feel full, helping us eat less, providing energy, and giving us amino acids, which are the building blocks of our bodies. The desserts in this cookbook are filling, real, whole food.

29. **CHILD-FRIENDLY SWEETS.** As a nation of unhealthy eaters, we must do better to safeguard the health of our young children, who are increasingly sick with preventable illnesses. This stevia cookbook is proud to be friendly to your child's health so that you can truly eat dessert without guilt.

30. **RECIPE ADAPTATIONS.** We all have our favorite treats and desserts. To help you along your journey toward a healthy kitchen makeover, I have included instructions on experimenting to adapt your family's beloved recipes in order to make them guilt-free.

31. **PASSION FROM SOMEONE WHO HAS BEEN THERE.** I am passionate about creating authentic health—real healthy kitchen makeovers—so that our good health can free us to influence the world for good, starting with our families and communities.

THE STEVIA DISCOVERY

At first glance, the stevia plant doesn't look like anything special. Most people, when asked to guess what kind of herb it might be, surmise that it's mint. It's a good guess, because the leaves do look like spearmint, peppermint, or even lemon balm.

The original discovery of stevia is unknown. The plant grows wild in certain parts of Paraguay. The local Guaraní people have gathered the leaves from the wild for centuries, at least. They use stevia to sweeten their yerba mate herbal drink, which is still immensely popular today in that region of South America.

The famed Portuguese adventurer Aleixo Garcia was among the first, if not the first, European to taste what the Guaraní called the "honey leaf" plant. In 1516, Garcia and others were exploring an estuary on the border of Argentina. While heading back to Spain, Garcia's ship crashed, and he was stranded with the Guaraní, with whom he'd previously had contact. After his shipwreck, he lived among the Guaraní for the next eight years.

From the days of those conquistadors, use of stevia as a sweetener began to spread. But it hasn't been until recently that stevia has commanded the attention of the whole world.

Stevia began to gain its modern global fame at the end of the nineteenth century when an intrepid Swiss scientist and explorer named Moisés Santiago Bertoni fell in love with Paraguay. Bertoni was perhaps the last of the true Renaissance men. His curiosity about the natural world was insatiable. He is most famed for discovering and classifying thousands of new plant and bug species and leaving behind a huge collection of more than 7,000 botanical specimens and 6,500 insect specimens that is still preserved and studied today. Bertoni himself might be most surprised to learn that among his most famous and lasting contributions is the research he did on stevia. He was the first to isolate the sugary metabolite called *stevioside* from the leaves of the plant and the first to imagine its commercial potential. Little could he have known that decades after his death, his work with stevia would lead to a huge, international love affair with this all-natural, calorie-free, nonglycemic sweet leaf.

World War I and World War II diverted scientific attention away from stevia, with good reason. Just as Bertoni was doing his work, the world was perfecting the process of refining sugar from beets and sugarcane. Sugar beet farming became a huge industry, and for the first time in the history of the world, sugar was cheap, plentiful, and easily available.

Let me mention that the world *nearly* began to take stevia seriously in World War II after a German blockage cut off England's supply of sugar. According to David Richard, author of *Stevia Rebaudiana: Nature's Sweet Secret*, the director of the Royal Botanical Gardens at Kew commissioned a study on whether stevia could be used in place of sugar. The study said yes, and England ordered stevia seeds from Brazil and

Freshly harvested sugar beets from a commercial sugar beet farm in Europe.

began growing the plant for the first time. Unfortunately, when the war ended, England went back to sugar and abandoned stevia.[1]

It wasn't until the 1960s that the movement toward healthier sugar alternatives burgeoned. Professor Osamu Tanaka, working at Hiroshima University in Japan, led the group that first isolated stevia's second major sugary metabolite, called *rebaudioside*. Japan was keen for healthier sweets, becoming perhaps the first nation in the world to worry that artificial sweeteners, such as saccharin, might be linked to cancer. In the 1970s, the Japanese government became the first in the world to approve all-natural stevia and stevia extracts as safe food additives. In 1971, the Japanese company Morita Kagaku Kogyo Co., Ltd. produced the world's first stevia extract for home and commercial use. The Japanese have prized stevia and used it widely ever since—it is even used to sweeten Coca-Cola in Japan as well as many other drinks and candies. Today, stevia is said to make up 50 percent of the sweetener market in Japan.

As more and more scientific research was performed on stevia, more countries fell in love with this sweetener, using it to sweeten gum, candy, coffee, tea, and soda. In Europe and the United States, stevia gained

Stevia extract in liquid form.

a growing grassroots following. The United States finally gave official approval for stevia as a food additive in 2008, followed by the European Union in 2011. Since then, stevia has exploded in popularity as a sugar alternative. Today, stevia blends and brands are given major space on the shelves of Walmart and grocery stores across the United States.

And this brings us to our use of stevia in our own kitchens today. Because it is a tricky ingredient, many Americans struggle to make stevia work in their favorite recipes. But here in this book, we are working to write the next chapter of stevia history by changing the way that we see and eat sweets. For anyone looking to give their kitchen, family, food, and health a makeover—without sacrificing sweets, treats, or desserts—this stevia cookbook is the place to start.

Welcome to a whole new way to love the sweet life.

1. David Richard, *Stevia Rebaudiana: Nature's Sweet Secret* (Bloomingdale, IL: Blue Heron Press, 1996).

THE SWEET HEALTH HOME MAKEOVER

give a lot of speeches and teach a lot of classes, and I like audience participation. To jump-start people into thinking seriously about a healthy home makeover, I like to start with a joke.

"Is there anyone here who has children, or knows a child, or has ever met a child? Please raise your hand," I say as my opener. And when everyone's hands are up: "Now keep your hand up if you like those kids. Does anyone here like their children?"

Of course, everyone laughs and keeps their hand up. But I have something up my sleeve.

"If you love your kids," I say mischievously, "obviously you wouldn't feed them anything that will, you know, slowly kill them. So let's take a quiz."

I invite you, dear reader, to take the quiz too.

1. In 2005, a team of scientists working with the US National Institutes of Health called a press conference to announce that our children and grandchildren will be the first in the history of the United States to have a shorter life expectancy than their parents because of their eating habits.[1] Think of it like this: we are giving them a shorter life span by teaching them, in their youth, habits that will slowly feed them to death. Keep in mind that type 2 diabetes is preventable for nine out of ten victims and caused solely by what we put in our mouths. Are you feeding them with their long-term health in mind?

2. Consider soda, apple juice, a drink mix, and an energy drink. Which is healthiest? Which is least healthy? I contend that the least healthy drink is the apple juice. Why? Because apple juice has a higher glycemic load than soda and energy drinks. Yes, it's true: a diet of apple juice has a terrible effect on your child's blood sugar, causing a greater spike than soda, believe it or not. You can see the comparative glycemic loads of any food or drink online. Now, instead of a high volume of sugar in your child's drink, can you imagine a protein-fortified Kool-Aid substitute with no sugar rush and no risk of turning your healthy child into a sick, diabetic adult down the road? (You'll find that recipe within this book.)

3. If ten-year-old children are obese because of what they have put in their mouths, is their obesity the fault of the ten-year-olds or the parents? I ask this question because there can be no solution, no healthy home makeover, until you realize who is responsible for your child's health. Your child's school is not in charge,

nor is their teacher, their friends, the government, television commercials, or even your family doctor. Most importantly, the child is not in charge. The person who must decide to change is *you*.

4. If your child is obese, how likely is it that you, the parent, are fit and trim? It is not always true, but I have noticed that most of the time, if a child is dangerously overweight, so is at least one parent. Children learn how to eat from their parents. If you are demonstrating a fit and trim life, you are teaching your child one thing. If you are guzzling soda and spending sums of money on sugar and fatty garbage food, you can't be shocked if your children are unhealthy.

5. Last question. If you want to do better, what do you do now? The answer: make sustainable change. There are ways to sabotage yourself, an interesting form of self-deception which I see as a growing trend. That is to jump in stupidly, trying to do everything all at once. Sustainable change is what counts. Choosing to reduce store-bought treats and desserts is a simple start. Using this stevia cookbook to make your delicious desserts healthy—without "diet food" flavor—is a sustainable place to start.

Welcome to a sweet kitchen makeover.

1. "Obesity Threatens to Cut U.S. Life Expectancy, New Analysis Suggests," National Institutes of Health, March 16, 2005, http://www.nih.gov/news/pr/mar2005/nia-16.htm.

THE SUGAR CRISIS

We have nowhere to get away from sugar.

Take, for example, Xander, my nine-year-old grandson. His karate teacher rewards him and the other students at the end of class by allowing them to choose a treat or two from a huge tub of cheap candies. Same thing for five-year-old Ada, Xander's sister, at the end of her dance class each week. When they go to the doctor for their shots, they are rewarded by getting to choose a

candy. In school, they are rewarded with candy. At church, their teachers give them sweet treats. We give them treats for their birthdays and, many times, for no big reason at all. I'm not even going to mention what happens at Halloween, Easter, and Christmas. They know they can ask for a sucker at the bank. Xander knows exactly which of my wife's coworkers have candy bowls at their desks. These kids love to make cookies with me in our kitchen. They beg for Kool-Aid, grab the after-dinner mints at restaurants, and make a beeline for the soda machine in restaurants if they are allowed. They get dessert in school lunch. At a recent Cub Scout activity, the reward was cupcakes with a swirl of frosting two inches high. The previous month, they handed out glazed donuts.

As adults, our lives are no less filled with sugar. Finding someone with an office job today who does not have sugar stashed somewhere in their desk is pretty rare indeed. At my local supermarket, I am greeted with a huge display of fresh-made donuts and cookies as soon as I walk in the door. The aisle of soda is far larger than the display of vegetables. The candy aisle is just as long as the soda aisle.

We wake up in the morning and put sugar in our coffee or drink sugary juice. We have soda with lunch and likely a sweet drink with dinner. Many of us have soda or energy drinks between meals to get us through the day. And if you want a challenge, try to find a breakfast cereal without sugar in it. Even the so-called "healthier" cereals are laden with sugar; they are called "healthy" only because they have a bit less sugar than what my friend calls the "choco-sugar-marshmallow puffs," which are squarely advertised to our children.

Have a midmorning lull? Help yourself to the office vending machine, where there is not likely to be a healthy choice—and if there is, we are not likely to choose it. After-lunch fatigue? Raid the candy stash in your desk.

This is just a short list of the obvious ways that our lives are flooded with sugar daily. Much of our sugar intake is less obvious. Ketchup—loaded with sugar. Packaged foods—often laced with sugar. Canned soups, bread, chips, barbecue sauce. Yogurt is packed with sugar—especially those marked "low fat" or "no fat." Sweet and sour sauce, pasta sauce, dipping sauce, salad dressing. Many protein bars,

The sugar crisis isn't limited to fast food. "Healthy" packaged foods like yogurt and canned fruit often contain high amounts of sugar.

granola bars, and "energy" bars have the same amount of or more sugar than a candy bar. New varieties of fruit, like apples and clementines, have been hybridized or genetically altered to greatly increase the amount of natural sugar in them. Canned fruit often has sugar added in the form of the syrup it's packed in. Deli food is boosted with sugar, from the glaze on the chicken or pork to the coleslaw. Bottled tea and store-bought green smoothies can have more added sugar than soda.

The McDonald's website lists sugar as an ingredient in *every single burger and sandwich* the company sells (at the time of this writing).[1] The Bacon Clubhouse Crispy Chicken Sandwich contains 16 grams of sugar—the same as half a package of M&Ms candy![2] The sugar content in most fast food burgers and sandwiches is startling.

Pizza is no better. According to the Domino's website, there is sugar in the crust, sugar in the sauce, sugar in the cheese. A barbecue pizza has as much sugar as a whole package of M&Ms candy.[3] Domino's is just an example; most pizza has a similar story.

Milk contains natural sugar, and milk substitutes contain sugar—soy milk, coconut milk, cashew milk, almond milk (though some brands offer an unsweetened option). Trying to find the sugar on food labels can be hard; companies can legally call sugar by scientific names, including dextrose, modified starch, glucose syrup, sucrose, maltose, fructose, lactose, honey, ribose, saccharose, monosaccharide, di-saccharide, polysaccharide, corn syrup, high fructose corn syrup, and others. Any of these can mean "sugar" when you see them on a label.

Sugar lurks everywhere. And even if you are the unheard-of person who does not eat sugar, you are still paying for it. The *Washington Post*, in a scathing 2013 editorial, reported that the federal government paid out $280 million in sugar subsidies in fiscal year 2013 alone.[4] How do we subsidize the price of sugar with our tax dollars? Well, the federal government gives sugar producers hundreds of millions of dollars in loans, secured by actual piles of sugar. When cheap Mexican sugar (subsidized by the Mexican government) floods the US market, the US sugar producers abandon their sugar collateral and keep the taxpayer cash. The government then sells the actual sugar at a huge loss. The whole thing has been created as a way for us, the taxpayers, to subsidize the price of sugar.

Meanwhile, a Bloomberg editorial published in 2013 titled "That Sickening Sugar Subsidy" reported that because of artificial government price supports, we in the United States actually pay a higher price for sugar than the market price; US companies have convinced the government that the real price of imported sugar is, ironically, too low and should not be allowed.[5]

THE SUGAR CRASH

We aren't innocent. We know we eat too much sugar—three times more than we should, according to health officials. We know sugar is bad for us.

Or do we?

Most people have a sense that the sugar in our food is up to no good. Many of us are concerned about sugar. We think about cutting the amount of sugar we eat. We make—and break—New Year's resolutions about sugar.

But how many of us can actually say *why* sugar is bad for us?

If you asked a hundred random people on the street, the answer you'll likely get is that sugar should be avoided because of calories. "Those sugar calories are bad for us," they will say. They might even use words like "empty calories" or "junk food." But many foods have way more calories per 100 grams than sugar: oil, butter, peanut butter, and chocolate, for example. Meat, dried fruits, and fruit juices have nearly identical amounts of calories per 100 grams as plain table sugar. Stigmatizing sugar strictly because of calories doesn't add up. It is true that sugar can be associated with "empty calories" or "junk food," meaning those calories may not be combined

with the critical protein, fiber, minerals, and vitamins that are naturally found in fruits, nuts, vegetables, meats, and grains. But accusing sugar of being "empty calories" is often arbitrary and, actually, the least of our worries when it comes to the dangers of overeating our favorite pick-me-up.

Scientifically speaking, sugar itself is not pure evil—we must have sugar to live. We just eat too much. Way too much. There is probably enough natural sugar in dairy and grains alone for our needs, let alone fruit.

So what is wrong with sugar? And why can't most of us, if asked on the street, name what is really dangerous about sugar?

As I write this, I have a friend sitting in a hospital more than a thousand miles away with her critically sick three-year-old daughter. Her daughter stopped breathing because of pneumonia and infection and, days later, has not yet been able to breathe on her own. They are far from home because this tragedy struck while on vacation. We'd like them to be home soon, safe, sound, and taking deep breaths. My friend has described her sedated three-year-old as "a puffy little Stay Puft," because her daughter's body is extremely swollen right now.

Our amazing human bodies balloon like this in times of crisis—a natural part of healing. Acute inflammation is often part of the body's response to infection or serious injury. Swelling is caused because our blood vessels expand where the body is injured to bring more blood to the area. Because they expand, they begin to leak plasma proteins and fluid, which are trapped in the surrounding tissue. The injured or infected parts of our body begin to swell up like a balloon being filled with water. Doctors call this "acute inflammation" or "acute edema." When the infection or injury goes away, so does the swelling. Our bodies return to normal.

Sugar causes the same kind of inflammation, but instead of being acute and dramatic, it is a chronic, low-grade swell, often not visible to the naked eye, and the consequences to our health are astonishing. The problem with chronic inflammation is that getting rid of it is difficult unless we change how we eat and exercise. When chronic inflammation invades our bodies, it brings a host of consequences.

SUGAR AND NONALCOHOLIC FATTY LIVER DISEASE

One in three to one in five adult Americans now has a condition doctors call *nonalcoholic fatty liver disease* (NAFLD).[6] Our liver is the organ that processes fructose, which is the most common added sugar in the American diet. Fructose makes up 50 percent of common table sugar. Fructose is considered safe when it naturally occurs in fruit, because fruit contains two kinds of fiber (*soluble* and *insoluble*) that slow the digestion of fructose. (Soluble fiber, which can be dissolved in water, and insoluble fiber, which does not dissolve in water, are both necessary for a healthy digestive tract.) For example, if you eat a fresh peach, the fiber in the peach and the peach skin slows digestion.

This is the natural way of eating fructose. But when fructose is refined, isolated, and added to food that does not have fiber, it strains the capacity of the liver. Slow fructose digestion is what our liver is built to handle. Rapid digestion—that is, eating fructose without fiber—slowly damages the capacity of our liver to process fructose. For example, this happens when you eat a handful of chocolate chips. There is little fiber in chocolate chips, so the liver can become overwhelmed processing the fructose. Chocolate chips are more than 50 percent sugar, which means that a quarter of each chocolate chip is fructose.

Over time, the liver develops fatty deposits as a symptom of the strain of overuse. "In some people with nonalcoholic fatty liver disease, the fat that accumulates can cause inflammation and scarring in the liver. This more serious form of nonalcoholic fatty liver disease is sometimes called nonalcoholic steatohepatitis [(NASH)]," according to the Mayo Clinic.[7] People with NAFLD are unlikely to ever know they have a problem until the disease progresses to a more dangerous form. Liver failure is the final stage of NASH. Normally, this is a rare outcome, but in the past twenty years, there has been a frightening increase in the number of reported cases.

Nonaclcoholic liver cirrhosis, or severe scarring and damage, develops in 25 percent of liver steatohepatitis patients. Without a transplant, these patients will die. Since 1980, the average amount of fructose we eat has doubled. During that same time, cases of NAFLD and NASH have also doubled, and most people with NASH also have type 2 diabetes.

New research published on SugarScience.org shows that "approximately 6 million individuals in the United States are estimated to have progressed to NASH and some 600,000 to NASH-related cirrhosis." It is deeply concerning that "NASH is now the third-leading reason for liver transplantation in America. And it will become the most common if recent trends continue."[8]

More alarming still is this: 13 percent of children now suffer from NAFLD.[9]

In this stevia cookbook, I aim to dramatically reduce the potential for NAFLD and NASH by adding fiber to nearly every recipe. Here's how:

- **REAL FRUIT PUREE.** My recipes mix pineapple-pear puree with stevia to replace sugar. These fruits contain natural fiber, which slows the digestion of fructose, helping the liver safely do its job in a natural way.

- **WHOLE WHEAT PASTRY FLOUR.** With the single exception of Vanilla Controversy Cake, there is no white flour used in the recipes of this cookbook. Instead, white flour is replaced with whole wheat pastry flour, which is much healthier for our digestive tract and liver function because it contains all of the fiber naturally present in wheat kernels. White flour is glycemically damaging to our bodies because the fiber has been removed. Whole wheat pastry flour is a special kind of whole grain flour that has been extra-finely ground. This fine texture keeps all the fiber but removes the grainy texture of regular whole wheat flour, which can distract from the flavor of pastries and cookies.

- **ALMOND FLOUR.** This "flour" is simply blanched (skin removed) almonds that have been ground up. It is used in several recipes in this cookbook because it makes lighter, fluffier cakes and pastries. A quarter cup of almond flour gives you not only 12 percent of the daily recommended protein but also 12 percent of the daily fiber you need, helping slow the digestion of sugar, which means the liver can do its job better.

A HEALTHY KITCHEN MAKEOVER FOR THE LIVER

If you want to reduce the chance of you or your children developing NAFLD or NASH, here is the answer:

- Use stevia to replace sugar as much as possible, using the sweetening techniques in this book.
- Eat more whole grains, and use less white flour. Eat whole grain bread using natural yeast as much as possible.

SUGAR AND TYPE 2 DIABETES

Perhaps the most important thing this book can do is educate and protect the rising generation from type 2 diabetes. Let me explain why.

Glucose is a kind of sugar that our muscles and body tissues must have. A certain level of glucose must be available to our cells at all times. Using stored supplies from our food, the liver makes glucose when necessary.

Glucose cannot enter into or be used by our cells without the help of insulin. Our pancreas produces the insulin necessary for the glucose in our bloodstream to enter our cells. When we eat too much sugar, the pancreas is forced to pump out larger and larger volumes of insulin. This effort literally wears out the pancreas, resulting in inflammation and permanent damage. As the pancreas tries to heal itself, scar tissue is created, limiting the efficiency of the pancreas. Eventually, the pancreas creates less and less insulin.

"Instead of moving into your cells . . . sugar builds up in your bloodstream," reports the Mayo Clinic.[10] "Being overweight is a primary risk factor for type 2 diabetes. The more fatty tissue you have, the more resistant your cells become to insulin. However, you don't have to be overweight to develop type 2 diabetes."[11]

Because type 2 diabetes damages our blood vessels, the complications of people living with type 2 diabetes are horrendous—and all because of sugar. Here is a list of some of the complications that arise with type 2 diabetes:

- The tissues and organs are slowly and irreversibly injured. The likelihood of heart attack and stroke increases significantly, along with other heart and artery diseases.

- The flood of sugar stuck in the bloodstream damages our capillary blood vessels, which reduces the flow of blood to our nerves, causing permanent nerve damage. This begins as tingling in the fingers, toes, and limbs and can lead to permanent and total loss of feeling.

- Because our kidneys contain a huge number of capillaries, diabetes leads to kidney failure and can mean years of dialysis and the need for a kidney transplant.

- Eye damage can occur. Cataracts, glaucoma, and blindness can be the result of diabetic damage to the blood vessels in the eyes.

- Amputation is more likely. Damage to the feet is particularly severe. When the damage is too great, amputation becomes necessary.

- A person with type 2 diabetes will experience a reduced ability to heal. The entire body, including the skin, is less able to heal itself of even minor injuries. One of the early signs of type 2 diabetes is when people hurt themselves and find that healing is much slower than expected.[12]

The real heartbreak is that while the number of people falling victim to type 2 diabetes is rising alarmingly fast, the disease is preventable for most people, if not for everyone. It is largely caused by what we eat. Even people who may be genetically inclined to develop type 2 diabetes can dramatically slow the disease and lead a normal life if they control the sugar they eat in all its forms, including potatoes, white bread, and rice.

SUGAR AND BELLY FAT

Everyone seems concerned about belly fat these days. When we eat more fructose than we need for energy, our liver turns the sugar into fats called *triglycerides*. Our body then deposits some of this fat around the belly for storage. This fat is also deposited around our internal organs.

"Just as people who drink too much get a 'beer belly,' those who eat or drink too much fructose can get a 'sugar belly,'" reports SugarScience.org. "Fat cells that accumulate around your midsection send out disruptive hormonal messages that upset your body's normal chemical balance. Scientists are actively studying how these hormonal imbalances become implicated in a wide variety of diseases, including heart disease, stroke, diabetes, cancer and Alzheimer's disease."[13]

This cookbook helps reduce the potential for belly fat by adding significant fiber to most recipes. Here's how:

- **STEVIA.** Simply put, stevia does not contribute to belly fat in any way. This natural sweetener is not turned into fat by the body, making it a perfect replacement for fructose and other sugars.

- **REAL FRUIT PUREE.** The pineapple-pear puree used with stevia in these recipes contains natural fruit fiber that slows digestion, helping us to feel satiated faster and full longer. Feeling full is a natural, safe way to help reduce the amount of calories we eat. Natural fiber reduces belly fat by simply helping us feel full so we eat less. Most of the American diet is low in fiber. Potatoes, rice, white flour, and white sugar: none of these help us feel full, which means we want to keep eating. Natural fiber does the opposite: it helps us feel like we've had enough to eat, and we are full and happy.

SUGAR AND PANCREAS DAMAGE

The job of the pancreas is to produce chemicals called *enzymes* and insulin that our body must have to break down and process food. As stated in the previous section, eating too much sugar forces our bodies to create triglycerides. Having too much of these fats in our bloodstream can damage our pancreas, gradually reducing the capacity of the pancreas to create the enzymes we must have, causing a condition called *chronic pancreatitis*.

"Chronic pancreatitis is inflammation of the pancreas that does not heal or improve, gets worse over time, and leads to permanent damage," reports MedlinePlus, a service of the US National Library of Medicine and the National Institutes of Health. "When inflammation and scarring of the pancreas occur, the organ is no longer able to make the right amount of [specific] enzymes. As a result, your body may be unable to digest fat and key elements of food."[14]

A stevia-and-fruit puree replaces much of the sugar in recipes in this book, helping to protect the long-term health of your pancreas.

SUGAR AND METABOLIC SYNDROME

One of the least understood yet potentially most dangerous consequences of sugar is what the Mayo Clinic calls "a cluster of conditions"[15] or metabolic syndrome. It is important to note that having one or two conditions does not mean you have metabolic syndrome; all five must be present. The expert physicians at SugarScience.org define the five conditions as follows:

- Large waist size: 35 inches or more for women and 40 inches for men

- High triglycerides: 150 mg/dL or higher (or use of cholesterol medication)

- High total cholesterol, or HDL levels under 50 mg/dL for women and 40 mg for men

- High blood pressure: 135/85 mm or higher

- High blood sugar: 100 mg/dL or higher[16]

Three of the five conditions are directly linked to overeating sugar. Having metabolic syndrome is both a disease predictor and a disease marker. It means you are much more likely to fall victim to type 2 diabetes or cardiovascular disease, which are two of the world's most prolific killers. "Metabolic syndrome is primarily caused by obesity and inactivity," reports the Mayo Clinic.[17] "According to the American Heart Association, 56 million Americans have metabolic syndrome," reports SugarScience.org.[18]

By implementing the recipes in this book to substitute the use of sugar and aid the body in proper, slow digestion, you can reduce your overall susceptibility to at least three of the five conditions of metabolic syndrome.

SUGAR AND LIFE EXPECTANCY

Here is the most startling, most devastating symptom of sugar in our diet: it is literally killing us.

On March 16, 2005, the US National Institutes of Health called a press conference to announce that for the first time in US history, the rising generation was expected to have a *lower life expectancy* than their parents.

> Over the next few decades, life expectancy for the average American could decline by as much as 5 years unless aggressive efforts are made to slow rising rates of obesity. . . . The U.S. could be facing its first sustained drop in life expectancy in the modern era.[19]

This loss of life expectancy is the culmination of all the sugar-related conditions we have discussed here: nonalcoholic fatty liver disease, belly fat, pancreas damage, diabetes, and metabolic syndrome. As you can see for yourself, these diseases are often not self-contained boxes. Belly fat affects the pancreas and liver. Pancreas damage affects diabetes and metabolic syndrome.

In other words, our health is like a set of dominoes. Sugar can trigger one or two unhealthy conditions, which then trigger other conditions.

If we make over our kitchens, we can prevent the dominoes from collapsing.

Our own health is important, but our biggest goal and highest concern should be influencing the health of our children and grandchildren. As adults, we can work to change our habits and earn better health. But we should do everything we can to influence and protect the good health of our children and grandchildren.

There is no way to separate our obesity from our sugar- and calorie-laden diets. However, stevia and the other healthy ingredients in this book create desserts that are *far and away healthier* than our traditional desserts. Let no one discourage you; we can have delicious desserts and be healthy too.

1. "McDonald's USA Ingredients Listing for Popular Menu Items," McDonalds.com, effective July 10, 2015, http://nutrition.mcdonalds.com/getnutrition/ingredientslist.pdf.

2. Ibid.

3. "Domino's Pizza Nutrition Guide," Domino's IP Holder LLC, 2009, http://cache.dominos.com/homev8/docs/menu/dominos_nutrition_v2.21.00.pdf.

4. "U.S. Sugar Subsidies Need to Be Rolled Back," *Washington Post*, November 25, 2013, http://www.washingtonpost.com/opinions/us-sugar-subsidies-need-to-be-rolled-back/2013/11/25/6082490a-53af-11e3-9fe0-fd2ca728e67c_story.html.

5. "That Sickening Sugar Subsidy," Bloomberg.com, March 13, 2013. http://www.bloombergview.com/articles/2013-03-13/that-sickening-sugar-subsidy.

6. Ariel E. Feldstein, Marsha H. Kay, and Naim Alkhouri, "Non-Alcoholic Fatty Liver Disease (NAFLD)," American College of Gastroenterology, January 2006, updated December 2012, http://patients.gi.org/topics/fatty-liver-disease-nafld/.

7. "Diseases and Conditions: Nonalcoholic Fatty Liver Disease Definition," Mayo Clinic, April 10, 2014, http://www.mayoclinic.org/diseases-conditions/nonalcoholic-fatty-liver-disease/basics/definition/con-20027761.

8. "The Toxic Truth," SugarScience.org, http://www.sugarscience.org/the-toxic-truth/#.VZMLgesqsRY.

9. Ibid.

10. "Diseases and Conditions: Diabetes Causes," Mayo Clinic, July 31, 2014, http://www.mayoclinic.org/diseases-conditions/diabetes/basics/causes/con-20033091.

11. "Diseases and Conditions: Type 2 Diabetes Risk Factors," Mayo Clinic, July 24, 2014, http://www.mayoclinic.org/diseases-conditions/type-2-diabetes/basics/risk-factors/con-20031902.

12. Author, "Article title," Website/Company, Date Written, URL.

13. "The Toxic Truth," SugarScience.org, http://www.sugarscience.org/the-toxic-truth/#.VZMLgesqsRY.

14. Todd Eisner, "Medical Encyclopedia: Chronic Pancreatitis," MedlinePlus, updated February 10, 2014, http://www.nlm.nih.gov/medlineplus/ency/article/000221.htm.

15. "Diseases and Conditions: Metabolic Syndrome Definition," Mayo Clinic, August 22, 2014, http://www.mayoclinic.org/diseases-conditions/metabolic-syndrome/basics/definition/con-20027243.

16. "Too Much Can Make Us Sick," SugarScience.org, http://www.sugarscience.org/too-much-can-make-us-sick/#.VaQ1qosqsRZ.

17. "Diseases and Conditions: Metabolic Syndrome Causes," Mayo Clinic, August 22, 2014, http://www.mayoclinic.org/diseases-conditions/metabolic-syndrome/basics/causes/con-20027243.

18. "Too Much Can Make Us Sick," SugarScience.org, http://www.sugarscience.org/too-much-can-make-us-sick/#.VaQ1qosqsRZ.

19. "Obesity Threatens to Cut U.S. Life Expectancy, New Analysis Suggests," National Institutes of Health, March 16, 2005, http://www.nih.gov/news/pr/mar2005/nia-16.htm.

TRUTH VERSUS INTERNET TROLLS: IS STEVIA DANGEROUS?

The Internet is full of nonprofessionals being paid to give "advice" and "information." Anyone can start a blog, write clickbait, and make a living. *Clickbait*, for those new to the Internet, is any title or link or teaser that is designed to be shocking or eye opening or intriguing enough to get you to click a link. If you click the link, the blogger or website owner gets paid through ad revenue. They must have huge traffic to their website to make money. So they create sensational, exploitative content that is now widely derided for lacking accuracy and substance.

If you type "Is stevia bad for you" into a search engine, you will find a list of blogs and other nonsense where people are being paid (through ad revenue on their blogs) to scare the wits out of you. None of it is true.

Let me be emphatically clear, as clear as I can be: *none of it is true*.

Based on intensive and rigorous scientific study, stevia and/or stevia extracts have been officially approved for use in food, as dietary supplements, and for human consumption in the United States, the European Union, Japan, and many other nations.

Here is the truth: in all the centuries that stevia has been used by humans, there is not one single documented case of anyone being harmed by it—not one person. But there are millions of cases of people being harmed by and dying from complications of eating excess sugar and morbid obesity. Stevia is the solution, not the boogeyman.

Below are a few of the clickbait pseudofacts about stevia that pop up online. Please forgive me if you sense a little attitude as I refute these false statements.

1. **STEVIA IS DANGEROUS BECAUSE IT IS HIGH IN OXALATES (OXALIC ACID).** First, here is a list of foods that are high in oxalates: blackberries, blueberries, raspberries, strawberries, kiwi, purple grapes, figs, tangerines, spinach, quinoa, almonds,

cashews, peanuts, soy, wheat, and chocolate. Second, oxalates are present in the human body at all times. Third, the human body converts vitamin C into oxalic acid, so if you are afraid of oxalates, you should avoid vitamin C as well. Fourth, there is no good evidence that stevia is high in oxalates. And, finally, it would be nearly impossible for anyone to be harmed by stevia because if you use more than a tiny amount of stevia, your food wouldn't taste good; no one recommends you use more than small amounts. Even if stevia were extremely high in oxalates, you would have to eat vast amounts of it to be in any danger. With respect, this whole argument is pure nonsense. And, by the way, oxalates are rendered harmless through cooking.

2. **STEVIA IS PART OF THE RAGWEED FAMILY, AND SO MANY PEOPLE ARE ALLERGIC TO RAGWEED.** This could not be more nonsensical. People are not allergic to ragweed; they are allergic to ragweed pollen. I myself am extremely allergic to ragweed pollen. Stevia does not produce or contain ragweed pollen, and you needn't fear having an allergic reaction even if you are allergic to ragweed pollen.

3. **STEVIA CAUSES A BLOOD SUGAR SPIKE IN SOME PEOPLE, BUT NOT OTHERS.** False. This could not be scientifically true because it is not possible for substances to cause blood sugar spikes in some people and not others. Tens of thousands, if not millions, of diabetics who regularly use stevia and test their blood sugar can tell you flat out that this is not true. What is true, however, is this: some stevia products contain fillers that will spike your blood sugar. I do not recommend using any of these products. Any stevia product that requires you to use more than tiny amounts in a recipe has fillers. Use either the pure leaf, or the 90 to 95 percent strength of pure extract of the leaf.

4. **STEVIA DOESN'T CONTAIN GLUCOSE AND THEREFORE DOES NOT HELP THE LIVER PRODUCE GLYCOGEN (GLUCOSE STORED BY THE BODY FOR LATER USE).** Yes, it is true that stevia does not contain glucose. It is false that this absence is harmful to us. In truth, it is not just helpful—it is the reason that stevia is the solution. This is why I suggest using stevia; particularly in the American diet, we eat so much sugar that it is actually damaging the liver, as discussed earlier in this book.

5. **STEVIA FEEDS CANDIDA.** Candida is a huge genus of yeasts, and some of the species in this genus cause infections in the human body, particularly in women. The number one cause of candidiasis (yeast infection) is likely antibiotic use, followed by poor personal hygiene, obesity, birth control pills, and diabetes. Now, to be clear, the human body cannot function without good bacteria and yeasts. But there is overwhelming scientific evidence showing that when we wipe out

the good bacteria and yeasts (through over-use of antibiotics), we are in clear and present danger of being colonized by bad bacteria and yeasts, especially *Candida albicans.* Also keep in mind that yeasts feed off of natural sugars. Stevia has a sweet flavor but contains no natural sugars, nothing that can feed candida. And, truly, sugar is not the issue when it comes to candida. Antibiotics and poor diet are what allow the good bacteria and yeasts in our body to die, leaving the opportunity for candida to colonize.

6. **STEVIA IS A CONTRACEPTIVE.** Absolutely not true. If you are using stevia to keep from getting pregnant, you might quickly find yourself pregnant!

7. **STEVIA WILL HURT YOUR ADRENAL GLAND.** The argument is that if your mouth tastes something sweet that doesn't actually contain sugar (like stevia), then your body is tricked into preparing for a sugar surge that never comes. The truth is this: studies have shown that our bodies don't react to flavors; they react to the molecular and nutritional content of our food. So eating sweet stevia will not cause the body to react as it would to sugar.

8. **STEVIA FORCES YOUR BODY TO RELEASE STRESS HORMONES BECAUSE OF HYPOGLYCEMIA.** This is an offshoot of the "stevia will hurt your adrenal gland" argument. The truth: stevia simply does not cause hypoglycemia, as you will see evidenced in clinical studies that I will cite later on. The whole argument is false.

9. **STEVIA WILL SUPPRESS YOUR IMMUNE SYSTEM.** False. Sugar causes inflammation, which taxes the immune system. There is no evidence that stevia suppresses the immune system. In fact, the evidence points strongly to the opposite.

10. **STEVIA INCREASES INFLAMMATION.** There is no source anywhere that shows this to be true. What we know for sure is that actual sugar causes dangerous, chronic inflammation.

11. **STEVIA LOWERS OR DAMAGES THYROID FUNCTION.** Again, there is absolutely no evidence to support this. This is based on the false claim that stevia causes hypoglycemia, which we've already established is not true.

12. **STEVIA CONTAINS GLYCERINE.** It is true that some liquid extracts of stevia that you can buy are made with glycerine. Glycerine (also spelled *glycerin*) is a sweet, thick liquid that is extracted from vegetables or petroleum. Pure vegetable glycerine is used in herbal medicine because of its extractive power. A homemade liquid extract of stevia can be made using either vegetable glycerine or alcohol (and you can even do a weak extraction in milk). Personally, I don't use liquid

stevia extracts unless I make them myself. For the purposes of this book, as explained earlier, I suggest either pure powdered stevia leaf, which you buy or grow and prepare yourself, or powdered extract of 90 to 95 percent purity, which is the highest purity available.

13. **SOME STEVIA PRODUCTS CONTAIN UNDEFINED "NATURAL FLAVORS."** If you buy stevia or stevia extract, instead of stevia-based products, this is not an issue. Product manufacturers are allowed by law to list "natural flavors" to describe minor ingredients on a list of ingredients to protect their recipes from being stolen. There are many stevia-based drink flavorings that contain citric acid, powdered lime or lemon, and other natural flavors. None of these are used or recommended in this book, because you can use pure stevia and real lime juice or lemon juice just as easily and far more cheaply.

14. **STEVIA IS A HORMONE.** No, stevia is not a hormone. Stevia is a green herb plant. Some people on the Internet say that "stevia has a hormone structure." No, stevia has a molecular structure, just like every other thing on earth. Stevia is not a hormone, and there is absolutely zero evidence that stevia produces anything like a hormonal reaction in the human body. Stevia is absolutely safe, as you will see in the upcoming scientific studies.

15. **STEVIA CAN BE TOXIC TO SOME.** Absolute nonsense. The argument online is that stevia lowers your blood sugar so much that it can kill you. This is purely made-up nonsense. No one has ever died from eating stevia. In all the centuries that stevia has been used by humans, there is not one single documented case of anyone being harmed by it—not one person. Stevia does not raise blood sugar, nor does it lower blood sugar. That is the point of stevia!

16. **STEVIA LOWERS BLOOD PRESSURE.** There is some clinical evidence that this is true, but the same clinical evidence also says that stevia never lowers blood pressure that is normal or already low, as you will see in the upcoming studies.

17. **PEOPLE CHOOSE STEVIA BECAUSE THEY ARE AFRAID OF CALORIES AND NATURAL SOURCES OF SUGAR, WHICH IS NOT EMOTIONALLY OR PHYSICALLY HEALTHY.** I don't even know what to say about this, it is so ludicrous. We who use and love stevia are afraid of diabetes, chronic inflammation, morbid obesity—all the bad things that excess sugar causes. People who are looking to improve their diets and health are not emotionally or physically crippled.

18. **NATURAL SUGARS IN GENERAL ARE A BETTER CHOICE THAN STEVIA.** In moderation, natural sugars, as found in fruits and vegetables, are good. However, natural

sugars are causing huge health problems in the United States and globally because we eat way, way too much of them. Stevia, alternatively, is an all-natural sugar-flavored leaf that offers sweetness in small doses and without the harmful effects.

19. **STEVIA EXACERBATES YOUR ADRENAL FATIGUE.** There is zero evidence that stevia has anything to do with adrenal fatigue.

20. **THE POWDER OF GROUND STEVIA LEAVES IS UNBEARABLY BITTER.** This is true if you are using too much of the powder and not using it correctly, as explained in this book.

21. **STEVIA WILL MAKE YOU EAT MORE CANDY AND DESSERTS.** Stevia does not make you crave sugar. When we take responsibility for our health, and the health of our children, everything changes, including our cravings.

22. **STEVIA IS SOMETIMES PROCESSED WITH CHEMICALS.** Creating an "extract" of anything is a process, usually involving alcohol, because alcohol is natural and better at food and plant extraction than any other natural substance known to man. Even vanilla extract is made with alcohol. But you don't have to buy processed stevia. You can use the whole leaf or the leaf powder or grow your own stevia and even make your own homemade extract following the recipes in this book. If you can't find a manufacturer that you trust, you will have no other choice but to grow your own stevia. I use both my own homegrown leaves and homemade extract, and I use and sell manufactured extracts and stevia leaves from stevia farms.

23. **STEVIA IS BAD FOR YOUR TEETH.** No. Cavities are caused by bacteria fed by sugar and by chewing ice, which creates microscopic cracks in the enamel of teeth and gives access to the bacteria that feed on sugar. Stevia, like birch sugar (xylitol), is a great way to help avoid cavities because neither one of them feed the bacteria that cause cavities.

STEVIA HEALTH

S o far, I've explained why sugar does not support health and explained, in part, why stevia does not have those same negative effects. Now I offer the facts of how stevia does indeed support health.

1. **STEVIA HAS NO CALORIES OR CARBS.** This is because stevia is a leaf and has highly concentrated sweetness. A quarter teaspoon of the full-strength extract of stevia leaves has roughly the equivalent sweetness of one cup of traditional sugar! Because stevia is used in such small amounts, it is considered to have no calories and no carbohydrate effect on the body.

2. **STEVIA PROTECTS AGAINST TYPE 2 DIABETES.** Overwhelming the pancreas with traditional sugar slowly wears out the ability of this critical organ to produce insulin, causing type 2 diabetes. Stevia does not require insulin for digestion and so does not tax the pancreas. Since 1992, there has been a 33 percent increase in the number of children diagnosed with type 2 diabetes, which used to be called "adult onset diabetes" because it was so rare in children. Using stevia in your kitchen will help protect the lives of you and your loved ones from this vicious disease.

3. **STEVIA IS ANTI-INFLAMMATORY.** Traditional sugar causes chronic inflammation in our joints, organs, and tissues that strongly contributes to degenerative diseases including heart disease, diabetes, joint pain, asthma, and much more. Stevia has none of these effects, and when used as a sugar substitute, it prevents the inflammation traditional sugar would have caused.

4. **STEVIA MAY PREVENT CAVITIES.** Experts report that studies at both Purdue University and Hiroshima University in Japan show stevia helps "retard plaque on teeth and suppress [bacterial] growth," according to SteviaCanada.com.[1] In 1990, Dr. R. Elton Johnson Jr., who grew up around stevia in Brazil, gave a presentation to the Calorie Control Council. "Under contract to us, Purdue University's Dental Science Research Group has done three special studies," one showing that stevia "'significantly' inhibits plaque growth" and another showing stevia users experienced a "20 percent reduction in cavities."[2]

STEVIA SCIENCE

For detailed statistics and assertions, I offer this information from the International Journal of Food Sciences and Nutrition:

- The extract from the green stevia leaves is a "natural herbal sweetener with no calories and is over 100–300 times sweeter than table sugar."

- "Stevia does not have the neurological or renal side effects of other artificial sweeteners."

- "Stevia is safe for diabetics, as it does not affect blood sugar levels."

- "Stevia possesses antifungal and antibacterial properties."

- "Mild stevia leaf tea offers excellent relief for an upset stomach."[3]

According to Stevia.com:

- Stevia "effectively regulates blood sugar and brings it toward a normal balance."[4]

- "Studies have . . . indicated that stevia tends to lower elevated blood pressure but does not seem to affect normal blood pressure. It also inhibits the growth and reproduction of some bacteria and other infectious organisms, including the bacteria that cause tooth decay and gum disease."[5]

- "Stevia is an exceptional aid in weight loss and weight management because it contains no calories and reduces one's craving for sweets and fatty foods."[6]

Below are some specific studies that demonstrates the health benefits and safe use of stevia.

Study 1

TITLE: "Overview: the history, technical function and safety of rebaudioside A, a naturally occurring steviol glycoside, for use in food and beverages."[7]

CONCLUSION: Stevia extract has "no negative effects on general health associated with doses equivalent to a 150-pound person drinking more than 2,000 8-ounce servings of a rebiana-sweetened [stevia] beverage. No treatment-related effects on any organ, including kidneys and male reproductive organs. No negative effects on general health, reproduction, growth, or development of adults or their offspring. No significant blood pressure effects in healthy subjects with normal or low-normal blood pressure. Did not affect blood sugar control and was well tolerated in people with type 2 diabetes. This paper summarizes the information used to conclude that high-purity rebaudioside A (rebiana) produced to food-grade specifications and according to Good Manufacturing Practices is safe for human consumption under its intended conditions of use as a general purpose sweetener."

Study 2

TITLE: "Safety evaluation of certain food additives: Steviol glycosides."[8]

CONCLUSION: This broad study showed that stevia extracts are nontoxic, help reduce weight, reduce hypertension, prolong life span, and may inhibit skin cancer.

Study 3

TITLE: "Antihyperglycemic effects of stevioside in type 2 diabetic subjects."[9]

CONCLUSION: Stevia reduces blood sugar spikes in people with type 2 diabetes.

Study 4

TITLE: "Stevia (*Stevia rebaudiana*) a bio-sweetener: a review."[10]

CONCLUSION: "We conducted a systematic literature review to summarize and quantify the past and current evidence for Stevia. We searched relevant papers up to 2007 in various databases. . . . Stevia can be helpful to anyone."

Study 5

TITLE: "A critical review of the genetic toxicity of steviol and steviol glycosides."[11]

CONCLUSION: Stevia poses no risk of genetic damage or mutagenic damage to humans.

Study 6

TITLE: "Antidiabetic activity of medium-polar extract from the leaves of *Stevia rebaudiana* Bert. (Bertoni) on alloxan-induced diabetic rats."[12]

CONCLUSION: Stevia lowers blood sugar without causing hypoglycemia, revitalizes the pancreas, and works better than some diabetes drugs.

Study 7

TITLE: "*In-vitro* Antimicrobial and Antitumor Activities of *Stevia Rebaudiana* (Asteraceae) Leaf Extracts."[13]

CONCLUSION: In some instances, stevia extract kills *Candida albicans*, is nontoxic to normal cells, and also had both anticancer and antiproliferative activities against cancerous cells.

1. "Stevia Research and Studies," SteviaCanada.com, http://www.steviacanada.com/studies.html.

2. R. Elton Johnson, "Stevioside, 'Naturally'!" Presented to The Calorie Control Council, November 6, 1990, http://www.cookingwithstevia.com/steviosides.html.

3. S. K. Goyal et al., Stevia (Stevia rebaudiana) a biosweetener: a review," International Journal of Food Sciences and Nutrition, February 2010, Vol. 61, No. 1, Pp.1–10.

4. Lisa Jobs, "A Better Alternative to Sugar and Artificial Sweeteners," Stevia. com, excerpted from *Sensational Stevia Desserts* (Valley Forge, PA: Healthy Lifestyle Publishing LLC, 2005), http://www.stevia.com/stevia_article/ stevia_a_better_alternative_to_sugar_and_artificial_sweeteners/8111.

5. James May, "Stevia—Sweetener of Choice for Future Generations," Stevia.com, http://www.stevia.com/Stevia_article/Stevia_Sweetener_of_Choice_for_Future_Generations/2413.

6. Ibid.

7. M.C. Carakostas et al., "Overview: the history, technical function and safety of rebaudioside A, a naturally occurring steviol glycoside, for use in food and beverages," *Food and Chemical Toxicology*, July 2008, Vol. 46, Supp. 7, Pp. S1–S10.

8. D. J. Benford, et al., "Safety evaluation of certain food additives: Steviol glycosides," World Health Organization, 2009, Pp. 183–219, http://whqlibdoc.who.int/publications/2009/9789241660600_eng.pdf.

9. S. Gregersen, et al., "Antihyperglycemic effects of stevioside in type 2 diabetic subjects," *Metabolism*, January 2004, Vol. 53, No. 1, Pp. 73–76.

10. S. K. Goyal et al., Stevia (Stevia rebaudiana) a biosweetener: a review," International Journal of Food Sciences and Nutrition, February 2010, Vol. 61, No. 1, Pp.1–10.

11. D. J. Brusick, "A critical review of the genetic toxicity of steviol and steviol glycosides," *Food and Chemical Toxicology*, July 2008, Vol. 46, Supp. 7, Pp. S83–S91.

12. Himanshu Misra et al., "Antidiabetic activity of medium-polar extract from the leaves of *Stevia rebaudiana* Bert. (Bertoni) on alloxan-induced diabetic rats," *Journal of Pharmacy and Bioallied Sciences*, April–June 2011, Vol. 3, No. 2, Pp. 242–248, http://www.ncbi.nlm.nih.gov/pmc/articles/PMC3103919/.

13. Sathishkumar Jayaraman, "*In-vitro* Antimicrobial and Antitumor Activities of *Stevia Rebaudiana* (Asteraceae) Leaf Extracts," *Tropical Journal of Pharmaceutical Research*, December 2008, Vol. 7, No. 4, Pp. 1143–1149, http://www.bioline.org.br/pdf?pr08037.

WHERE AND HOW TO BUY STEVIA

There are a lot of stevia-based products in grocery stores and health food stores today, but before you take one home, it is *essential* to ask two questions:

✓ 1.   Are there added ingredients?

✓ 2.   Is the stevia powder extract 90 percent strength or more?

ARE THERE ADDED INGREDIENTS?

Read the ingredients list. Most stevia on the market is actually a "stevia blend"—which means it is stevia mixed with other sweeteners, some of them artificial, some of them not.

And because stevia has very little bulk, be very suspicious anytime you see large boxes or bags marked *stevia*. If you do see large packages, read the ingredients list—to bulk these up so they can be used cup for cup as a sugar replacement, they often contain maltodextrin, which is a starch derivative that adds significant calories to stevia and, worse, spikes the glycemic index. There is no benefit to buying a stevia blend with these added ingredients in them.

IS THE STEVIA POWDER EXTRACT 90 PERCENT STRENGTH OR MORE?

If maltodextrin has been added, is the blend at least 90 percent stevia? Don't be fooled by blends with low amounts of stevia and lots of maltodextrin or, if the extract is a liquid, lots of water. Infuriatingly, most stevia extracts don't label the percent strength on the bottle or box. There are two ways to tell if stevia is 90 percent when the label does not say:

1. Under *Supplement Facts* on the label, look at the number of *Servings Per Container.* If the container is between 3 and 5 ounces, the *Servings Per Container* should be 1,000 to 2,000 or more. Anything lower means you likely have a blend high in maltodextrin and low in stevia extract—usually one part stevia extract to four parts maltodextrin!

2. Look at the price. A typical 3.5-ounce bottle of powdered stevia extract will cost about $20 (at the time of this writing). If you find a bottle for half that price, it is likely to be 25 percent strength extract, which means it has a huge amount of added maltodextrin and you will need to use at least four times as much to get the same result—which will add calories and glycemic impact to your food (because of the maltodextrin).

Buy only pure stevia leaf powder (pure, ground-up leaves of the stevia plant) and pure stevia extract. If a stevia extract is less than 90 percent strength, it almost always means that huge volumes of maltodextrin have been added as an unnecessary bulking agent.

The sweetener Truvia was the first stevia-based sweetener blend to be mass-produced in the United States. Originally, it was available only in single-use packs for coffee drinkers and was quite expensive. The price has begun to come down a little, and Truvia now offers a sugar-stevia blend for baking.

Luckily, in 2011, health food stores began to offer stevia extract in both liquid and powdered forms. The liquid form is less useful for baking and in some cases may contain alcohol (like real vanilla extract).

My favorite brand of 90 percent stevia extract discontinued sales of its 95 percent product in 2013 and started selling blends with a lot more filler maltodextrin instead, which sent me for a scramble. The solution? I finally had to start sourcing my own bulk, guaranteed-pure stevia leaf powder and guaranteed 90 percent strength stevia extract powder. People attending my stevia baking classes asked to buy my guaranteed-strength stevia, and by popular demand I now sell it on my website, SeedRenaissance.com.

I believe I am the only seller anywhere to offer 90 percent strength stevia extract powder in small amounts (and low prices), which is ideal for anyone looking to try stevia for the first time or to experiment with stevia in baking and cooking. I've also used the KAL brand, which at the time of this writing sells stevia extract powder online and in health food stores for about $23 for 3.5 ounces and 2,381 servings per container.

You can look online and in your local health food store for other brands that meet the criteria listed above or use a brand with lower stevia extract, keeping in mind that you will have to use 4–5 times more than is listed in the recipes in this book.

LIQUID STEVIA EXTRACTS

Like powdered extracts, the problem with liquid extracts is that strength (percent of stevia) varies wildly and is rarely explained on the label. To make matters worse, some stevia extracts contain alcohol and some don't. Every brand of liquid extract seems to be different. For these reasons, I stick with guaranteed 90 percent strength powdered stevia extract, because the consistency of the extract is crucial for making stevia work in baking. Because liquid extracts are usually low or weak in their stevia strength and vary so much, I don't use them unless I make them myself at home with my homegrown leaves (see "Homemade Vodka Stevia Extract" on page 74 for my Homemade Vodka Stevia Extract recipe or "Homemade Milk Stevia Extract" on page 75 for my Homemade Milk Stevia Extract recipe).

BACKYARD STEVIA

started growing stevia in 2009. In warm climates, stevia is perennial, but where I live on the cold bench of the Rocky Mountains, stevia has to be kept over the winter inside my geothermal greenhouse. (For information about geothermal greenhouses, see my book *Backyard Winter Gardening: Vegetables Fresh and Simple, In Any Climate, Without Artificial Heat or Electricity—The Way It's Been Done for 2,000 Years.*)

It took me several years of trial and error to figure out the secrets of growing stevia from seeds:

- Grow seeds in the house. The greenhouse is simply too hot.

- When you are initially planting the seeds, simply press them to the soil. Don't bury them at all.

- Start the seeds in a container with no drain holes. I start the seeds in a simple kitchen bowl in some compost soil. These seeds are so sensitive to drying out that they must be moist at all times.

- Water the seeds and seedlings with warm water, never cold water.

- Be very gentle when watering the seedlings—pouring water on the plants can dislodge the root, damaging or even killing the baby plant.

- Be patient. Stevia seeds are going to be slow. They will either be slow to germinate or slow to grow. Sometimes the seeds take up to three weeks to germinate. I find that if I start them in the house, they germinate within a week but they grow slowly; it can take another two or three weeks before the second set of leaves (called the *true leaves*) appears.

- Keep the seedlings out of direct sunlight. They like part-sun to shady environments.

- If the plants look like they are suffering, my friend Linda Smith gave me a great tip—put a plastic bag

over them. We live in Utah, where there is little humidity, and putting a plastic bag over the whole planting pot raises the humidity and helps the plants. (If you live in a place that has constant humidity, you likely won't need to put a bag over the pot.)

- Stevia seeds don't germinate in temperatures lower than 65 degrees. And if the temperature is too high—like in a greenhouse—then the top of the soil can dry out; this seems to kill the seeds. If the seeds dry out even once after they are planted, they will likely never grow.

Starting stevia plants from seeds can be hard. But don't despair, even if you don't have a green thumb. There is an easier way. I got my first stevia plant from a grower at the local farmers' market, and now, four years later, even our local greenhouse sells them. Buying live stevia plants has become much easier, and once you have a live plant, you simply take three- to four-inch cuttings of the stems and plant them to create new plants. Strip all the bottom leaves, and bury most of the stem in the soil. Then abide by all the tips above as if you were starting seeds. I have successfully used this method and even given starters to friends this way.

Stevia plants never grow large—in my garden, they are about a foot tall—and in the heat, they go to flower fairly quickly. At most, one plant produces roughly fifty small leaves. These leaves can be dried and ground up for use in baking, but using the whole leaf does not work as well as using the extract. Although I continue to grow stevia in my garden and experiment with it, it would be easier to buy stevia extract in order to have enough for everyday baking and cooking.

Finally, a note on saving stevia seed from your own plants: Stevia seed is extremely susceptible to genetic bottlenecking, which means that seeds should be saved only from large populations of plants grouped together. For true seed with a good germination rate, you would need pollination from at least several hundred plants, which is not practical for backyard seed savers. If that is too daunting for you and your backyard garden, don't feel bad about buying true seed.

You can purchase true stevia seed from my online seed company, SeedRenaissance.com.

STEVIA Q&A

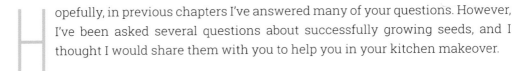

Hopefully, in previous chapters I've answered many of your questions. However, I've been asked several questions about successfully growing seeds, and I thought I would share them with you to help you in your kitchen makeover.

Q: I recently opened a stevia seed packet. I am hoping the dust was the seeds. Does the dust need light to germinate? I dusted some seedling mix lightly over the top of the soil.

A: Stevia seeds are naturally small. Stevia seeds should be pressed into, not buried in, the soil for best germination. You should keep the seeds in only partial light.

Q: I am having trouble getting from stevia seeds to plants. Do I have bad seeds?

A: Stevia seeds do not age well. Germination begins to fall rapidly if the seeds are older than two years.

Q: I can get the seeds to germinate, but they seem to die when I move them outside.

A: Transfer seedlings outside only after the last frost. Stevia will not grow much in hot summer weather, but will suddenly grow rapidly in the autumn. When the plants have grown, harvest as soon as flower buds appear—cut stems to about two inches tall, and dry leaves for kitchen use. Stevia must be harvested before the first frost. Bring the plant indoors to winter on a sunny windowsill, and this plant will be perennial. One common reason that people think their stevia plants, whether indoors or outdoors, are dying is because stevia is only a root perennial. This means that all stevia plants die back completely in winter. If the roots freeze, the plant will die. If the plant is indoors and dies back, the plant is not dead; it has just gone seasonally dormant. You must continue to regularly water your indoor stevia plants even after they die back, and you must leave the plant in a sunny window. The plant is not dead and will produce new shoots and leaves in spring.

Q: I've never had actual stevia leaves. Do they have that super sweet taste and then leave a bitter taste in your mouth like the stevia drinks that you buy at the store?

A: It depends. When I give garden tours, I give people a tiny piece of a stevia leaf to suck on. With stevia, the amount is critical. You can suck on a whole leaf and taste the sweetness. But if you start to chew on a leaf, the sweetness intensifies. I have never tried to chew up a bunch of leaves, but I can only imagine that they would be bitter. You have to get the amount right. We are so used to thinking about sugar in terms of cups that it is hard for us to transition to thinking about stevia in tiny amounts.

Q: I am starting my stevia plants from seed and want to make sure I plant enough. How many plants are enough?

A: Of course, the answer depends on how much stevia you use in a year. One stevia plant can produce perhaps 1/4 pound of dried leaves or more. I try to keep six to eight plants or more.

Q: Spider mites are killing my stevia plant; how can I kill them without harming the stevia?

A: Spider mites or any pest should not be allowed to remain on houseplants. To kill spider mites and most indoor or outdoor plant pests, use a 50 percent concentration of Caleb's Edible Weedkiller Recipe, available at SeedRenaissance.com. However, if your plant looks like it is dying and is not severely infested with mites, it is likely that the season, autumn or winter, is to blame, and your plant is simply going dormant.

INCREASING STEVIA SWEETNESS

Stevia has a natural sweetness, but it is not exactly like sugar, and it isn't much like brown sugar. When you are making adjustments to classic and favorite recipes, there are a few ways to highlight the sweetness and re-create those same flavors by combining our leading lady, stevia, with other delicious ingredients.

STEVIA AND PINEAPPLE

The anise-like aftertaste of stevia vanishes when combined with the correct amount of fresh or canned pineapple. Stevia has a great relationship with all citrus fruits; citric acid helps remove the bitterness and increase stevia's flavor forgiveness range. This relationship really shines when it comes to pineapple. Mixing the right amounts of stevia with pineapple puree gets rid of the bitterness that comes when stevia is used incorrectly. But too much pineapple can skew the flavor of many recipes, so I add a little pear to the puree and the recipe flavors are just right.

STEVIA AND COCONUT PALM SUGAR

Stevia does not brown or caramelize like traditional white sugar, which can change the flavor and texture of some recipes. I discovered that I could use stevia combined with small amounts of coconut palm sugar to impart the flavor, texture, and color of brown sugar or caramelized sugar to a recipe. Coconut palm sugar is made from the sap of coconut trees. It is a 100 percent sustainable product with a natural brown-sugar flavor and half the glycemic index of traditional sugar, in addition to a bounty of natural minerals and vitamins, which you don't get with traditional sugar. There are other sugar substitutes on the market, including yacon syrup and brown rice syrup, that can give a similar flavor, but they have a lot more calories than traditional sugar, ounce for ounce. In this book, you will find that I use small, responsible amounts of coconut palm sugar combined with stevia to give a brown-sugar or caramelized-sugar taste and texture without sacrificing the healthy qualities of my recipes.

STEVIA AND BIRCH SUGAR

Birch sugar is generally called *xylitol*. It is a sugar substitute made from the fiber of birch trees, other hardwood trees, and corncobs. Xylitol is a naturally occurring substance with an extraordinary history. Anyone who has read my *Forgotten Skills* series of books knows that there is a special place in my heart for the people who suffered through World War I and World War II, honing the self-reliance of whole nations. Cut off from the world, Finland had no way to domestically produce sugar during World War II and no way to import sugar because of the war. Birch sugar had been discovered by German and French scientists in the late 1800s. Finland had birch and other hardwoods and began experimenting to make its own self-reliant sugar during the war.[1]

Today, the process of extracting natural sugar from trees has been perfected. This sugar is present in low amounts in the fiber of many fruits, vegetables, and even mushrooms. The human body also produces a small amount of xylitol each day. It is an all-natural sweetener found in large enough amounts in hardwood trees and corncobs that it can be refined for commercial and home cooking.

What I'm about to say might seem like a petty point, but the name kept me from using this sugar for years. Xylitol gets its name from the Greek word *xylon*, meaning "wood," but I didn't know that. Xylitol just sounded fake, creepy, and unappetizing to me—like something cooked up by evil robots in a factory somewhere. It wasn't until I learned about the Finnish history of making this sugar during the war that I finally came around. I still hate the name, and in this book, I'm going to insist on calling it *birch sugar*—because that is what it is. I hope the whole world, and all the manufacturers, will join with me, even if their xylitol comes from other hardwoods or corncobs. Birch sugar is simply a better name.

Birch sugar's health benefits are huge and should not be ignored. Birch sugar has no negative effect on the body's glycemic index, making it far safer for our health than traditional sugar.[2] Even better, birch sugar has one-third fewer calories than traditional sugar. It does not feed the bacteria that cause cavities. Small clinical studies have shown birch sugar may even help remineralize the damaged or worn enamel of teeth.

There is one downside to birch sugar: it is broken down by specific, naturally oc-curring enzymes in our bodies. Manufacturers claim it can be used cup for cup to replace traditional sugar in recipes. Personally, I find this claim is not helpful; many health enthusiasts will tell you that it causes stomach upset and flatulence when used cup for cup. This is because while the body naturally produces this sugar and the enzyme to break it down, it is hard for the body to immediately ramp up enzyme production to digest these new, large amounts. In this book, I solve this problem by using birch sugar only in small amounts and almost always combined with protein powder, which slows digestion and has its own health benefits.

When we combine stevia with other natural ingredients, like citrus, coconut palm sugar, and birch sugar, the overall sweetness of stevia stands out and makes our recipes closer to the traditional flavor we have come to expect.

1. "The History of Xylitol in Finland," Peppersmith, May 31, 2015, http://www.peppersmith. co.uk/2015/05/the-history-of-xylitol-in-finland/.

2. "FAQs," Xyla, 2013, http://www.xylabrands.com/en/xylitol-landing-page/consumer-home/ faqs/?ref=binfind.com/web.

THE APPLE PROBLEM

"You can never get enough of what you don't need, because what you don't need can never satisfy you." —Dallin H. Oaks

Have you ever longed for a fresh apple?

In her journal, my great-grandmother Lexia Warnock recalled yearning for apples. In 1896, when she was six years old, she wrote, "we waited very impatiently for the Early Joe apples to begin ripening. We played games of our own manufacture in the black currant bushes, and picked gooseberries and greengages for canning for winter, but the nicest of all were the early apples." Her grandmother, Ane Marie Dastrup, had an apple tree in her yard that Lexia loved. "One tree was a joy of our childhood," she wrote. "The apples were small, yellow, and sweet. We loved to go to Grandma's after school and get our pockets full of them."

To young Lexia, 120 years ago, fresh apples were a rare luxury.

Today, we can go to the store and buy apples twenty-four hours a day, any day of the year. To us, apples are ordinary. No one yearns for apples the way Lexia did, waiting "very impatiently" for them to ripen. To Lexia, apples were a sugary special occasion.

When sugar becomes a special occasion food, and when we develop the cravings for naturally balanced foods—like sweet fruit with lots of fiber—then we will be satisfied. Until then, we keep looking for those things that *can't* satisfy us. For example,

we might eat only raw veggies for a few months, then become a sugar celibate for a few years, then go paleo, or South Beach, or follow this celebrity diet or that one. We can cleanse, juice, starve, eat only this, only that. We can alphabetize our dieting sins, scrapbook them, be angry, be depressed. We can spend money on this plan and that program. But these deprivations and diets, while they seem to meet some of our physical needs and help us lose weight, fail to fulfill our cravings. We are not making permanent life changes that result in permanent happiness. The truth is that we want to eat sugary treats and we want to do so without guilt and without harming our bodies. We want to eat delicious desserts and have them fill us.

Instead of embarking on another fad diet, change who you think you are and how you think; then you can permanently become a different, better, happier self. The only way to create change is to start asking yourself hard questions.

Here are some questions to get you started:

- What can I do today that will change me for the better?

- What can I do to give myself more control over my life?

- What can I do to create greater influence?

- What can I do to create confident finances (not wealth, not riches, but confidence that I will be self-sufficient, that I will have what is sufficient for my needs)?

- What can I do to create abundance for myself and those around me?

- How can I influence my own health and my body and take responsibility for my sicknesses and weaknesses?

- What can I do to pave the correct and safe and sufficient path forward for my kids and grandkids?

- What can I do to keep myself from being swayed by the winds of confusion and the fads that seem to batter the world constantly? How can I be the deeply rooted tree that is not twisted, broken, or crippled by storms?

- What do I need to study?

- How can I discern between conflicting opinions with confidence?

- How can I trust my sources?

- Am I on the right path? Am I walking alone? Am I leading or following?

- Am I present?

After you have asked yourself these hard questions and others, you will be able to see two important things:

1. What you really have.

2. What you really want.

Now you can compare what you have to what you want, create a goal, and begin an action plan. You will have a vision of change in your life and a plan to make the change happen.

Once you can envision how you really want your life to be, start educating yourself about how to get what you want. I hope this book will be useful to you.

The change we make must be sustained and sustainable. Nearly every nutritionist and dietician agrees that yo-yoing your weight is perhaps as dangerous as being morbidly obese. Below are some ways to judge whether you are on the right path.

IS MY PATH EXEMPLARY?

Your path becomes much clearer when you know you are doing the right thing for your children—*you are showing them the right way.* If you are fat and miserable, the right way is to show them how to change. They are watching you and learning from you. You can teach them to be healthy. And if you have taught them something else, you can teach them to change. When they are healthy adults, they will bless you for giving them the foundation of health in their youth.

AM I ENERGETIC?

Energy is what it is all about. Energy is the only coin we can spend to buy achievement, to buy endurance. When you are sick, you are not productive. When you have no energy, you are not moving towards your goals. Your health is intimately involved in determining whether or not you have the energy to work toward your goals and support your family. When you are energetic, you are on the right path.

IS THIS FINANCIALLY SUSTAINABLE?

A short time ago, I was in a specialty grocery store and started speaking with a woman who had read some of my books. This woman said she loved my books because she and her family were trying to really improve their health and make important changes. Then she started asking me about a whole list of exotic "health foods." She wanted to know if I was taking an extract of this plant and that plant, if I was buying a particular trendy health food, which machine I was using. She was very excited to tell me about all the money she and her husband were spending on their quest for a whole new life.

Shelling out a fortune is rarely the answer. Local, sustainable abundance, with an emphasis on doing as much as you can to feed yourself from your garden, if possible, and cooking with fresh ingredients in your own kitchen, at the very least, is the answer.

Being wise with money is the basis of most good things in life—marriage, family, career. Remember above all, any change you make must be both *sustainable* and *sustained*. If you can't save yourself locally, then you will lose the war. When you change to a new way of eating, it cannot be a financial burden. Your health must be financially sustainable. This is one of many reasons I love stevia. I can grow it myself, or I can buy the extract and use such small amounts that stevia is truly inexpensive.

When you have a vision of what you want and clear plans to get there, you'll find power to make changes.

IS THIS PLAN PERSONAL?

You will never sustain someone else's plan. The food you eat has to be your responsibility and your joy. That doesn't mean that you shouldn't look far and wide for the best information—you should. If I have done my job right, this book will be useful to you. But food habits have to become your own, based on your goals and your vision. In this life, you only get what you want. My body has to be my responsibility, my accountability, and my desire. If I look at myself and wish for something else, I'm on the wrong path. If I look at myself with a vision and a plan to change, I am on the right path.

IS THIS HAPPINESS?

As I have mentioned, I was a sugar celibate for several years. I lost weight and took control of my diet by living each day with white knuckles, hanging on to my vow of sugar celibacy for dear life. But I was not happy. To be sure, I was happier with my body than I had been in years.

But I was not *happy*.

I lived in daily fear that I would fall off the no-sugar wagon. I feared every holiday, every pie, every container of ice cream, every package of candy, every picture of a dessert. Sustainable change must allow for true happiness. Deprivation is not the answer. There is another way, a natural way—the Stevia Solution. You can have healthy desserts. You can have the pleasure of sweet treats in a smart, healthy, responsible, and delicious way.

IS THIS ABUNDANCE?

Abundance is one of those words that is now entirely overused. The pursuit of abundance has become one of those psychobabble journeys, fraught with fake speech and nonsense. So forgive me for using it here.

Abundance is a real thing, if you approach it carefully. When it comes to eating, we can't feel caged, trapped, shorted, jailed, put upon, or punished. None of this is abundance. We also can't be fat. Obesity is not abundance; it is a plague, a disease, a misery that gets harder and more horrible as you age.

Sugar addiction is not the path to abundance. Neither is sugar celibacy or any kind of plan that forces you to spend the rest of your life counting calories with white knuckles or journaling every morsel you put into your mouth. Sure, those are ways of taking inventory of who we truly are, and they might be a good starting place for

Think carefully about your future. What do you want your life to look like years from today?

change. But life can't be abundant if you feel like you are always being watched or tracked. Abundance must include health, energy, and good food. A dismal diet will always feel like prison.

WHAT WILL MY LIFE LOOK LIKE YEARS FROM TODAY?

Probably the single best way to know if you are on the right path is if you have invested days and months in it.

What does the life I want look like? Some people want to feel more confident in their clothes. Some people simply don't want diabetes. Some people want better control of arthritis or other inflammation.

Here is my personal vision: I don't want to go up a pants size.

For about sixteen years, this has been my one and only weight goal. After I lost fifty-two pounds, I vowed that whatever I did, however I did it, I would not go up a pants size. I am proud to say that sixteen years later, I still wear the same pants size. I wish I could go back to myself sixteen years ago and say, "You did it! It *is* worth it!" Because it has not always been an easy journey. Recently I realized that it might be time for a new goal. As you look through my new goals below, consider what you want yours to be.

- I want better coordination. I've never been a coordinated person. But lately my coordination has been going downhill. I want to arrest and reverse that trend with exercise and a fit body.

- I want to ski! I love it. I will never be a fast skier, and I will always stick to the easy runs, but as I age, I want to keep skiing.

- I want the energy to keep up with my grandkids. Well, at least partially. Let's be honest, no adult can keep up with young kids. But we do a lot together. We love to vacation with them, taking them to see all the great places around us. I must have the energy to keep up.

- I want to be healthy enough to heal. I am not a runner, I don't work out, and I don't go to the gym. But I am active—I hike, I have an extensive garden, and I ski. I need a body that can heal so that I can do the things I love.

- I want to eat primarily from my garden. And we do, most of the time, unless we are eating out. I love my garden, and I love fresh food. I love knowing that I grew the food and that, no matter what day of the year it is, I can eat fresh despite the snow and blizzards or blazing sun and drought. I do it because I want to save money and because I want to know where my food comes from, how it was treated, how the soil was treated, and how the earth was treated so that I could eat. I want confidence in our ability to care for ourselves on our land.

As you look through my new goals, consider what you want yours to be.

- I want a pastoral lifestyle. I want joy. Above all, I want peace. I want peace so that I can paint and write and love and be with family and friends. So that I can be useful. I don't want to be a burden on society, on an insurance company, on taxpayers, on my wife. That is not peace. That is not abundance. At the end of my life, I want to know I did everything possible to give health to my family and grandkids and the people who turned to my books. I want to know that I left the earth better than I found it, that I created both the peace and the space the next generations will need. When there is authentic abundance, there is peace.

- When I die, I want the people who knew me to say, "He led one of the most meaningful, useful lives in the history of the world. No one worked harder than he did to create health in the world."

I think it is also important to be specific and clear about what you don't want. As an example, here is my list of things I don't want:

- I don't want the little kids to grow up and say, "My grandfather and his generation shorted me, cheated me, selfishly took the best for themselves, and left us to fend for ourselves." I don't want them to say I and my generation created or contributed to problems and then left them to solve those problems.

- I don't want to leave debt to my kids and grandkids. I don't want to leave them without a moral compass. I don't want to fail to teach them how to be happy or how to discern what is real and valuable.

- I don't want my family to say, "I wish he hadn't been a burden to us," or "I wish he hadn't died before his time because he couldn't control what he put into his mouth."

- I will have failed if my wife ever has to say, "He isn't here for me."

- I don't want to waste time. Every hour I am unhealthy is an hour that I cannot spend passionately. Every hour that I am at war with myself is an hour that I cannot help others. Every ounce of energy that I must spend on correcting myself, healing myself, strengthening myself, worrying about myself, regretting, or loathing is energy that I cannot spend strengthening and lifting others.

By this point, you are probably thinking, *This guy has totally lost the thread of this book. This has nothing to do with stevia, nothing to do with dessert!*

But you would be wrong.

I am convinced that it is all tied together. When our food is real, when our health is real, our life is real.

Stevia is a step toward being real and being in control. Stevia is a step toward creating peace with my body and my love of food, the pleasure of eating dessert, and the joy of cooking in my kitchen. I find happiness in watching people love my food and eat every crumb, knowing that there is no guilt, no bad ethics, no harm being done.

I started this chapter with the quote: "You can never get enough of what you don't need, because what you don't need can never satisfy you."

Are you satisfied?

SURPRISINGLY SWEET, HONEST PROTEINS

You will find protein powder as an ingredient in many of the recipes in this book, including some that will surprise you. For example, my recipe for Sweet & Healthy Powdered Sugar Substitute uses protein powder. As you will see below, the health benefits of protein powders are staggering. However, there are three specific reasons to add protein to our foods and especially to our desserts:

1. Protein lowers the glycemic index and glycemic load, making sugars less dangerous to our health.

2. Protein is literally the building block of life. Protein breaks down into amino acids, which are what our bodies are made of. We must eat foods that break down into amino acids if we want to be healthy.

3. Protein takes longer to break down, which means we feel full longer, which in turn reduces the craving for sugar and food in general and helps us lose weight simply because when we feel full, we eat less.

PROTEIN SOURCES

Meat, eggs, and cheese provided life-sustaining protein for all our ancestors that came before us. But none of those people were as sedentary as we are, so their dietary needs were different.

Today, meat, eggs, and cheese have fallen out of favor in the health community because they are high in fats. Instead, plant, vegetable, or whey-based protein powders are sought after. Unfortunately, protein powders are subject to the whims of fad and fashion, and every year or two there seems to be a new powder in style.

The solution to all this is simple: don't buy brand-name protein powders. Instead, buy whole food protein powders made of one natural ingredient without additional "ingredients" mixed in.

Many commercial protein brands have been combined with many other ingredients because they are used for muscle gain or other athletic goals. In addition to the extra ingredients, these mixtures are also very expensive—$20 to $30 a pound or more. For home use, these are not the protein powders you want. You just want complete, natural, whole food protein powder, such as whey protein isolate, hemp powder, or a powder that is a mix of natural vegetable proteins. Try to avoid protein powders that have added flavors or any added ingredients.

I realize this may be controversial advice because protein powder mixtures are a huge business and people fall in love with certain brands or flavors, especially when using them in protein shakes or green smoothies. After all, the goal of advertising is to help build loyalty to brands and products, so the system is working. However, consider the benefits of eating a whole food instead of a proprietary protein mixture with added ingredients. Authentic natural foods, such as whey protein or hemp protein, are just whey (left over from making cheese) or hemp plant seeds (there are no mood-altering drugs in hemp seeds), and they are much cheaper than protein formulations. They are not "brands" or "miracle formulations," because they are not formulations at all—they are just one natural ingredient. However, if you have fallen in love with a certain protein mix brand, it is better to use that than nothing.

Here is a look at some whole food protein powder options.

Whey protein isolate

32 GRAMS CONTAINS:

- 25 grams of protein (50 percent of the daily recommended value)

- 1 gram of fiber (4 percent of the daily recommended value)

- 120 calories

Note: values may vary depending on brand and source.

BENEFITS OF WHEY PROTEIN ISOLATE:

- This vegetarian superfood (whey is a by-product of making cheese) is very high in protein.

- It is complete protein because it contains all twenty amino acids, which are the building blocks of a healthy body.

- It contains little or no fat or natural milk sugar (lactose).

- It naturally boosts immunity. Some of the proteins naturally found in whey are immunoglobulins, a molecule created by the human body and also naturally found in milk and whey, that the body must have for a healthy immune system.

- It is rich in cysteine and glutamate. These molecules are both used by the body to create glutathione, a potent antioxidant that is needed by the human body in times of stress and sickness.

- It is high in branched-chain amino acids, which help prevent muscle break-down as we age.

- It is high in the essential amino acid tryptophan, which naturally improves mood and sleep regulation.

- It contains glycomacropeptide, a natural "casein-derived 64–amino acid pep-tide" which "may help control and inhibit the formation of dental plaque and dental caries" (cavities) and help the body feel full after eating, according to WheyofLife.org.[1]

- It contains the glycoprotein lactoferrin, which inhibits the growth of bacteria and fungi in the body with its ability to bind iron.

- Whey is water-soluble, making it easy to add to recipes without changing the texture of the food.

- Whey is white in color, making it easy to add to recipes without changing the color of the food.

For information on this list, and to learn the science behind the health benefits of whey protein, visit the Whey Protein Institute at WheyofLife.org.

DOWNSIDES OF WHEY PROTEIN ISOLATE:

- It is low in fiber. Hemp protein powder is much higher in fiber, though it does not contain the same health benefits as whey protein, especially the immune-enhancing benefits. The solution to this problem is to use a mixture of whey and hemp protein powders in your cooking when possible.

- It is expensive. Whey protein isolate is $14 a pound in the bulk foods cold storage room at my local health food store. The good news: it is only necessary to use this ingredient in small amounts, so a few dollars' worth goes a long way. And buying five dollars' worth of protein powder is far cheaper than the cost of being chronically sick!

Hemp protein powder

30 GRAMS CONTAINS:

- 11 grams of protein (22 percent of the daily recommended value)

- 13 grams of fiber (52 percent of the daily recommended value)

- 130 calories

    Note: values may vary depending on brand and source.

BENEFITS OF HEMP PROTEIN POWDER:

- This vegetable, vegan superfood (made by grinding hemp seeds) is very high in protein.

- It is high in fiber, especially insoluble fiber, which is an essential prebiotic for natural probiotic gut growth.

- It is high in minerals (magnesium, iron, and zinc) and beneficial fatty acids.

- It is a complete protein because it contains all twenty amino acids, which are the building blocks of a healthy body.

DOWNSIDES OF HEMP PROTEIN POWDER:

- It has an undesirable color. This powder is dark green, and even a few table-spoons will give a green hue to your cookies, for example. There are two solutions to this problem. First, use it in naturally dark-colored foods, such as brownies or chocolate cake, where it is easy to hide. Second, become comfortable with green cookies and other baked goods. For individuals and families who are beginning their healthy home makeover journey, this may take some time. Most people who are more advanced on the healthy home makeover journey have become accustomed to the natural colors of authentic whole foods and are no longer bothered by it. I regularly make green chocolate chip cookies using the recipe in this book by using hemp powder for half the required protein powder. I also regularly make Sweet & Healthy Powdered Sugar Substitute with a light green hue by using hemp protein for one-third to one-half of the protein powder called for in the recipe. (I use whey protein for the remaining portion.)

- It is expensive. The hemp protein I buy is $11 a pound in the bulk cold storage room at my local health food store. The good news, again: you only use small amounts, so a few dollars' worth goes a long way. And I'll repeat this as well—buying a half pound of protein powder is far cheaper than the cost of being chronically sick!

Vegetable protein powder

30 GRAMS CONTAINS:

- varying amounts of protein

- widely varying amounts of fiber

- widely varying calories

Right now, vegetable protein powders are the hip new trend in protein, and the market has exploded with options. Every option is different, with the protein sourced

The market for vegetable protein powders has a myriad of options. Do your research and read the labels carefully.

from a huge array of plants and vegetables. The list of sources below, believe it or not, is just a short list, and new sources seem to become popular all the time.

- green and yellow peas

- brown rice

- chickpeas (garbanzo beans)

- ancient and modern beans and bean sprouts, including kidney beans, lentils, adzuki, flax, and more

- sacha inchi tree seeds

- ancient grains and grain sprouts, including quinoa, amaranth, millet, and buckwheat

- almonds, cashews, pistachios, and other nuts

- tempeh and tofu (both made from soybeans)

- plant seeds, including sesame, pumpkin, sunflower, poppy, and chia

- seitan, which is sort of an artificial meat made of wheat gluten

- unsweetened cocoa powder

- alfalfa

- coconut flour

- spirulina and chlorella (powdered dry algaes)

The benefits are too myriad to list because they change by ingredients, and each brand name vegetable protein powder on the market has a different mix. Some have more protein; some have more fiber. Avoid protein powders with added:

· salt

· sweeteners (including hidden sweeteners like brown rice syrup)

· chemical ingredients

· body-altering additives (for muscle bulking, for example)

Each vegetable protein source listed above has its own benefits, and each is sometimes associated with controversy about the way it is grown, imported, and processed. Do some research of your own and find the best and most naturally processed protein in your area.

1. "About Whey Protein: Whey Protein Components," WheyofLife.org, http://www.wheyoflife.org/
   components.

COMPARISON OF GLYCEMIC LOADS FOR COMMON FOODS AND INGREDIENTS

The numbers listed here represent the glycemic load (GL), not the glycemic index. The glycemic index of foods made salacious headlines in the 1980s and 1990s with stories claiming that watermelon, among other things, was killing people. Those stories have since been debunked, because glycemic index does not take into account several factors influencing the actual effects of sugar on the body. (In other words, watermelon is not dangerous.)

Keep in mind, however, that these glycemic load numbers are calculated when eaten alone after twelve hours of fasting. In real-life consumption, the glycemic load is much more complex. Proteins, fiber, and fat lower the glycemic load of small amounts of high-glycemic foods, but the glycemic load is exponential, meaning that the GL for a small amount of a food may be 50 but when eaten in large amounts at one time that number can go much higher. For example, as you will see below,

Coca-Cola has a GL of 14 to 16 when 250 grams are drunk, but the GL spikes to 30 when the amount is doubled.

These glycemic load numbers are therefore considered a baseline for good health with common-sense portions. Large portions of most foods are simply unhealthy and may spike the glycemic load.

HOW TO READ THE GLYCEMIC LOAD CHART	
Healthy	10 or less
Moderately unhealthy	11–19
Unhealthy	20 or more

Note: When a food listed below has a glycemic load range instead of a specific number, it is because different brands of the same food were tested and each gave a different GL result. Most of the testing for each food was done on 8–10 people or more. Data sources are listed at the bottom of the table.

NAME	SERVING SIZE	GLYCEMIC LOAD
Pear, raw	120 g	4
Pear halves, canned, in reduced-sugar syrup	120 g	4
Dove dark chocolate	50 g	6
Coca-Cola	250 g	14–16
Coca-Cola	333 g	20
Coca-Cola	500 g	30
Milk, full fat	250 g	3
Milk, skim	250 g	3
Peanuts	50 g	1
Microwave popcorn	20 g	7
Table sugar, white	40 g	26
Nesquik, made with 1.5% milk	250 g	5
Chocolate ice cream, 15% fat	50 g	4

Agave nectar	10 g	1
Fructose	10 g	1
Fructose	40 g	8
Glucose	10 g	10
Glucose	40 g	40
Clover honey	25 g	15
Lactose	10 g	5
Maltose	10 g	11
Maple syrup	25 g	10
Sucrose	10 g	7
Sweetened condensed milk	110 g	33
Xylitol (birch sugar)	10 g	1
Karo dark corn syrup	30 g	27
Lasagna noodles, boiled 10 minutes	180 g	26
Baked white potato, without skin	150 g	26
Baked white potato, with skin	150 g	19
Spaghetti (regular), boiled	180 g	20–22
White rice, boiled	150 g	23
Vanilla cake (packet mix), with frosting	111 g	24
Corn Flakes	30 g	21
Corn Pops	30 g	21
Pop-Tarts, double chocolate	50 g	25
Sweet corn, boiled	80 g	11
Carrot, raw	80 g	2
Cashews	50 g	3
McDonald's hamburger	95 g	17

McDonald's Filet-O-Fish	128 g	20
Orange juice	250 mL	12
Cranberry juice	250 mL	19
Apple, raw	120 g	6
Apple juice	250 mL	10–13
Apple juice, unsweetened	250 g	12
Carrot juice	250 mL	10
Watermelon, raw	120 g	4–5
Pineapple, raw	120 g	6
Pineapple, canned, in natural juice	120 g	9
Banana, raw	120 g	11–16
Raisins	60 g	28
Sirloin steak, mixed cooked vegetables, and mashed potatoes	360 g	35
Turkey cranberry sandwich on multigrain bread	200 g	34
Nutella spread	20 g	3
Peanut M&Ms	30 g	6
Milky Way bar	60 g	26
Skittles candy	50 g	32
Snickers bar	60 g	15–23
Ground beef over rice with an orange	300 g	24
White bread with butter	100 g	28
Kraft Macaroni & Cheese	180 g	33
Clif energy bar, cookies and cream	65 g	49
Clif energy bar, chocolate brownie	65 g	22

Stir-fry chicken and rice with cooked vegetables	360 g	55
POM pomegranate juice	236 g	21
Milk chocolate bar	50 g	12
Yoplait Light strawberry yogurt	200 g	10
Yoplait artificially sweetened strawberry yogurt	200 g	2
Greek yogurt, natural	200 g	1

Atkinson, F. S., K. Foster-Powell, and J.C. Brand-Miller. "International Tables of Glycemic Index and Glycemic Load Values: 2008." *Diabetes Care*, 2008. http://care.diabetesjournals.org/content/suppl/2008/09/18/dc08-1239.DC1/TableA1_1.pdf.

"The Sugar and Sweetener Guide." TheSugarandSweetenerGuide.com. http://www.sugar-and-sweetener-guide.com/glycemic-load.html.

"The Glycemic Index." The University of Sydney. Last updated August 8, 2014. http://glycemicindex.com.

TIPS FOR ADAPTING YOUR FAVORITE RECIPES USING HEALTHY TECHNIQUES AND INGREDIENTS

- Experiment by replacing one cup of sugar with one cup of pineapple-pear puree and one-fourth teaspoon of powdered stevia extract (90 percent strength).

- Pineapple-pear puree can be used to cut some of the butter or oil from a recipe. Start by trying to replace up to half of the oil or butter with an equal amount of puree.

- Sweet & Healthy Powdered Sugar Substitute (see "Sweet & Healthy Powdered Sugar Substitute" on page 77 for the recipe) can be used when you need a bright sugar flavor or a white sugar or when you are looking to cut calories and remove glycemic interaction. The whey in this recipe also adds protein, which helps flatten the overall glycemic load of a dessert.

- Use small amounts of coconut palm sugar when you need a brown-sugar or caramel flavor. This sugar has half the glycemic index of table sugar, making it a healthier choice than traditional brown sugar. However, I use it sparingly because this sugar option has nearly the same calorie count as traditional white sugar.

- Whole wheat pastry flour can be used to replace white flour because it has a much lower glycemic index and far more nutritional value. It is also a great source of prebiotic fiber.

- Almond meal flour can be used when you need a light, fluffy flour. Because whole wheat pastry flour is denser than traditional all-purpose white flour, almond meal flour can be used to help lighten the texture of a dessert. Almond flour is a good source of protein, which lowers the overall glycemic load of your dessert. Almond flour also has a light color, which helps when you are trying to make white cake, white frosting, white cookies, or other desserts that need a white color palette to be visually successful. However, be cautious because using too much almond flour can add a lot of calories to a recipe.

- Expect to do some tinkering. To adapt a recipe perfectly, you will likely have to try several versions, tasting each and making adjustments. This is because puree adds extra moisture and stevia does not replace the volume of sugar. In addition, you need much more stevia to sweeten one cup of oats, for example, than one cup of milk. Wheat flour needs more stevia; almond flour needs less.

STEVIA
STARTERS

STEVIA BASE
FRESH FRUIT VERSION

There has always been one problem with stevia—stevia can have a lingering, bitter taste. Through several years of experimentation, I have learned that the aftertaste of stevia vanishes when combined with the correct amount of fresh or canned pineapple. Citric acid helps remove the bitterness and increase stevia's flavor forgiveness range. Pineapple, particularly, works well with stevia. Mixing the right amounts of stevia with pineapple puree gets rid of the bitterness that comes when stevia is used incorrectly. However, too much pineapple can skew the flavor of many recipes. A puree of pears and pineapple, mixed with stevia in the right proportions, is a great way to replace sugar in recipes. This stevia, pineapple, and pear base—while unpalatable on its own—is the key to replacing sugar in sweet recipes. For the recipes in this book, use the puree as a healthy substitute for sugar, oil, and butter.

MAKES 3 CUPS STEVIA BASE

2 cups diced ripe pear, peeled and deseeded

1 cup diced ripe pineapple, skin and core removed

1 teaspoon powdered stevia extract, 90 percent strength

1   Pour the pears into a blender, cover with the blender lid, and blend until smooth. Pulse on a low gear, stopping between pulses to push down the fruit with a spatula and clear any air pockets that may form (air pockets halt the blending process). Continue this step until there are no large pieces of fruit and the fruit puree begins to swirl downward in the blender on its own.
2   Add the pineapple, then repeat the pulsing and pureeing from Step 1.
3   Add the stevia extract powder. Cover the blender and use the highest gear to liquefy the fruit puree. Depending on the power of your blender, this step may take 30 seconds to 2 minutes. You want to break down any strings in the pineapple into pulp. Use the base immediately in another recipe, or cover and store in the fridge for up to 2 days.

CANNED FRUIT VERSION

This is simply a variation of the previous recipe. Because it is so convenient, this is the recipe that I usually use. Following the other recipes in this book, use the puree as a healthy substitute for sugar, oil, and butter.

MAKES 4 CUPS STEVIA BASE

1 can (29 ounces) pears, in light syrup

1 can (20 ounces) of pineapple chunks, unsweetened, in 100 percent pineapple juice

1 teaspoon powdered stevia extract, 90 percent strength

1   Open the cans and drain away as much juice as possible.
2   Pour the fruit into separate bowls and check for anything inedible. (Don't trust it to be perfectly prepared—I have found seeds, pear skin, and stems in my canned fruit.) Remove any unwanted material and discard.
3   Pour the pears into a blender, cover with the blender lid, and blend the pears until smooth. Continue pulsing until there are no large pieces of fruit and the fruit puree begins to swirl downward in the blender on its own.
4   Add the pineapple, then repeat the pulsing and pureeing from Step 3.
5   Add the stevia extract powder. Cover the blender and use the highest gear to liquefy the fruit puree. Break down any strings in the pineapple into pulp. Use the base immediately in another recipe, or cover and store in the fridge for up to 2 days.

HOMEMADE VODKA STEVIA EXTRACT

Be aware that this extract will have a natural green hue, which will color some recipes. It may also have a slightly leafy flavor. Because this method does not extract as many of the flavor molecules from the leaves as commercial extracting methods, you will need to increase the amounts, by taste, called for in the recipes in this book.

MAKES 4 OUNCES EXTRACT

1 ounce dried* stevia leaves, crumbled or powdered (available at SeedRenaissance.com)

4 ounces good-quality vodka

1   Place the dried stevia in a glass jar. Pour the vodka over the stevia. Shake or swirl the jar to incorporate the ingredients.
2   Cover the jar with a lid and place it in a cupboard, away from sunlight, for at least 6 weeks, shaking or swirling the bottle once every few days.
3   After 6 weeks, strain the liquid through cheesecloth or voile cloth. Discard the crushed or powdered leaves, keeping only the extracted liquid.
4   Keep the extract in a dark glass jar, out of sunlight, for long-term storage. This alcohol extract will keep for years at room temperature.

Never use fresh leaves to make alcohol-based extract, as the leaves may go moldy or allow pathogen growth in the extract.

Like using vanilla extract, the alcohol in the stevia extract will be removed by most baking and cooking, but if you wish to remove the alcohol for making punch or other recipes, pour the extract into a pan on the stove on lowest heat. Bring to a boil, keeping the extract on the lowest heat possible, then turn off the heat when the alcohol has evaporated. You will know this has happened because the volume in the pan will reduce by half. Pay close attention, though, because this happens very quickly once the extract has heated up. Extract without the alcohol may go bad within weeks and should be kept refrigerated.

HOMEMADE MILK STEVIA EXTRACT

You can make stevia extract using milk instead of vodka, but the stevia strength will be considerably weaker than the vodka extract. You can also use water, which will make an even weaker extract, but it will have some sweetness.

Again, this extract will have a green hue that may color some recipes and might have a chlorophyll-like taste. It is also weaker than commercially produced extract, so you will have to at least triple the amounts called for in the recipes in this book.

MAKES 3 OUNCES EXTRACT

1 ounce dried stevia leaves, crumbled or powdered (available at SeedRenaissance.com), or 1 ounce clean, fresh stevia leaves

3 ounces whole milk or water

1 Put the stevia and liquid into a pan on the stove. Using low heat, bring the liquid to a boil. Boil for 1 minute, then turn off the heat. (Prolonged boiling can damage the sweet flavor).

2 Allow the mixture to cool. Strain with cheesecloth or voile cloth. Use the extract immediately, or refrigerate for 1–2 days.

HOMEMADE POWDERED STEVIA EXTRACT

This extract also has a natural green hue, which will color some recipes and may have a chlorophyll taste. Because this method extracts far less of the flavor molecules from the stevia leaves compared to commercial extracting methods, you will need to double or triple the amounts called for in the recipes in this book.

MAKES 1/2 CUP EXTRACT

3–4 ounces homemade stevia extract (vodka, milk, or water)

6 cups dry powdered milk granules, to taste

1   Pour the stevia extract into a bowl. Stir in the powdered milk granules until a thin paste is formed. The paste will be green.

2   Spread the paste as thinly as possible over a silicone baking liner on a cookie sheet or over parchment or waxed paper. (Paste that is too thick will be difficult to use later.) Securely cover the entire tray with cotton or voile cloth. Air-dry until completely desiccated, which will take 1–2 days or longer. (Drying in the oven is not recommended as it may affect the flavor of the powdered milk.)

3   Crumble the dry extract and store in a covered container for later use. (Powder that is not completely dry is not safe to store or use.) The crumbled powder may also be pulsed in a blender to create a finer powder.

SWEET & HEALTHY POWDERED SUGAR SUBSTITUTE

I'm proud to say that, to my knowledge, this is the only powdered sugar substitute in the world with significant protein, which is provided by the whey protein powder in this recipe. Beyond its huge health benefits, the protein powder is also necessary to help the blender more easily turn the birch sugar (xylitol) into a fine powder. The whey also helps to keep the birch sugar flavor from becoming cloy and helps the body digest the birch sugar more easily. As explained earlier in this book, birch sugar is a World War II invention of necessity: a sugar refined from the fiber of corncobs and birch trees that does not interact with the body's glycemic load and has one-third less calories.

MAKES 1 1/2 CUPS SUGAR SUBSTITUTE

1/2 cup protein powder

1 cup birch sugar

1   In a bowl, whisk the ingredients together thoroughly.
2   Pour the mixture into a blender.* Pulse on the lowest gear for 30 seconds. Stop the blender and stir the mixture with a butter knife. Then blend on the highest gear for 15-second increments or until the birch sugar granules have been reduced to powder. Do not overblend this recipe because overheating the gear base of the blender will cause the powder to melt and harden.
3   After emptying the powdered sugar substitute into a dry container for storage, thoroughly wash and air-dry your blender jar to avoid any sugar melting or hardening at its base.

It is important that your blender jar be completely dry to make this recipe. Any dampness inside the blender will cause the powdered sugar to clump and harden, especially around the blade assembly base.

For white powdered sugar, use whey protein isolate. For protein powder with fiber, use 1/4 cup whey and 1/4 cup hemp protein powder, but note that this version will have a light green hue. For full information on protein powder types and benefit, see "Protein Sources" on page 58.

SYRUPS, JAMS, TOPPINGS & FROSTINGS

SUGAR COOKIE FROSTING

The Sweet & Healthy Powdered Sugar Substitute used in this recipe has significant protein, which helps flatten the body's glycemic load. The fruit puree adds prebiotic fiber—making this the only sugar cookie frosting recipe in the world with both real protein content and prebiotic fiber. While it may not sound delicious, neither one affects the flavor or texture of the frosting. Additionally, this frosting is white *and* takes food coloring: no small feat for a healthy frosting recipe.

MAKES 2 CUPS FROSTING

1/2 cup Sweet & Healthy Powdered Sugar
    Substitute (see page 77)

2–3 teaspoons Stevia Base (see page 72)

1 1/4 teaspoons milk

1/3 teaspoon vanilla extract

Food coloring, if desired

1   Whisk together all the ingredients except the optional food coloring. Add an additional 1/2 teaspoon of the Stevia Base as necessary to make the frosting the consistency you want.

2   Add food coloring, if desired, 1 drop at a time.

> Depending on how finely you blended the powdered sugar substitute when you made it, this recipe might have a grainy texture. If so, heat the completed frosting in a heavy-bottom saucepan on the lowest heat possible, stirring until the grainy texture is gone (about 2–4 minutes). As soon as the frosting is smooth, turn off the heat, transfer the frosting to a bowl, and let it cool to room temperature before using.

ROYAL ICING

This royal icing has significant protein, prebiotic fiber, and smooth sweetness. Your body will love the low glycemic load as you indulge in your favorite desserts with this icing.

MAKES 2 1/2 CUPS ICING

2 cups Sugar Cookie Frosting (see page 80)   1 egg white, whipped to soft peaks

1   In a heavy-bottom saucepan, whisk together the frosting and soft peak egg white over lowest heat for 1 minute (just enough to cook the egg white).
2   Cool and use to ice cookies, or tint with food coloring as desired.

BUTTERCREAM FROSTING

This is not a true buttercream frosting; the fruit puree replaces some of the butter and cream while adding prebiotic, natural fiber, making this recipe healthier than buttercream frosting. The whey thickens the mixture and adds significant protein. It is a great spin on traditional frosting that your sweet tooth and your stomach can agree on.

MAKES 1 CUP FROSTING

1 tablespoon butter, room temperature, or cold coconut oil

3 tablespoons Stevia Base (see page 72)

1/2 tablespoon whey protein isolate

2/3 cup Sweet & Healthy Powdered Sugar Substitute (see page 77)

1/4 teaspoon vanilla extract

1 teaspoon cream

1   Whisk all the ingredients together until the consistency is smooth.
2   Add more Powdered Sugar Substitute if it is not sweet enough, 1/2 teaspoon at a time.

RICH CHOCOLATE FROSTING

The stevia-and-fruit puree significantly reduces the sugar and oil in this recipe, and you can adjust the rich flavor of the chocolate to suit your tastes.

MAKES 1 CUP FROSTING

2 tablespoons butter

1/3 cup Sweet & Healthy Powdered Sugar Substitute (see page 77)

1/4 cup Stevia Base (see page 72)

3/4 teaspoon vanilla extract

1 tablespoon powdered milk (plus 1 teaspoon if thicker frosting is desired)

Pinch of salt

1 tablespoon unsweetened cocoa powder

1–2 teaspoons additional unsweetened cocoa powder (optional, for dark chocolate frosting)

1   Mix all the ingredients together in a bowl using an electric hand mixer on the lowest setting.

2   Let the mixture sit for 2 minutes to allow the powdered milk to soften and begin to melt into the mixture.

3   Using the hand mixer again, start mixing at the lowest setting and gradually move to the highest setting. Mix until completely smooth, about two minutes.

4   Pour the mixture into a heavy-bottom saucepan over lowest heat. Bring to a boil without increasing the heat; this will take about 2 minutes. Then boil slowly for 3 minutes.

5   Remove from heat and cool completely before using.

CREAM CHEESE FROSTING

If you are like me, your idea of traditional frosting begins with a bag of powdered sugar. Wouldn't it be nice to swap that for something much healthier? You can! And you'll love the creaminess of this recipe. Use this frosting to ice either the chocolate cake or the brownies found later in this book.

MAKES 2 CUPS FROSTING

1 package (8 ounces) cream cheese

1/2 cup Sweetened Whipped Cream (see page 89)

1/3 teaspoon powdered stevia extract, 90 percent strength

1/2 teaspoon vanilla extract

1/3 cup Sweet & Healthy Powdered Sugar Substitute (see page 77)

1   Combine all the ingredients using an electric mixer. Mix in an additional pinch of stevia if you desire a sweeter frosting.

FLAVOR OPTIONS: Try adding a few drops of lemon, lime, or grapefruit essential oil (or whatever your favorite essential oil is). You could also add 1 teaspoon of chocolate mint syrup or any flavored syrups, or 2 teaspoons of pineapple juice, peach nectar, or apricot nectar. Or omit the vanilla and add instead the juice and zest of 1 lemon or lime for a citrus flavor.

CARAMEL FROSTING

If you desire the rich, dark sweetness of brown sugar and caramel in your desserts, this caramel frosting is the answer. The coconut palm sugar won't spike the glycemic load, and it rounds out the flavor.

MAKES ENOUGH FROSTING TO COVER AN 8X8-INCH PAN OF BROWNIES OR BARS; RECIPE CAN BE DOUBLED TO COVER AN 8X8-INCH CAKE

3 tablespoons Sweet & Healthy Powdered Sugar Substitute (see page 77)

2 tablespoons butter, softened

1 tablespoon coconut palm sugar

1/4 cup Stevia Base (see page 72)

1 Stir all ingredients together in a saucepan. On medium heat, bring the mixture to a full boil.

2 As soon as a full boil is reached, lower the heat by half. Stir the mixture continually for 2 minutes, then turn off the heat.

3 Transfer the caramel mixture to another dish. Allow it to cool for a few minutes, then place it in the fridge to set up and chill for at least an hour. Spread over brownies, bars, or cake.

MILK CHOCOLATE STEVIA SAUCE

The Stevia Base puree used in this recipe decreases the amount of oil without compromising the texture. Use this recipe as a dip for strawberries, to make the hot cocoa recipe found later in this book, or over ice cream.

MAKES 1 CUP CHOCOLATE SAUCE

1/4 cup olive oil or coconut oil

1/4 cup unsweetened cocoa powder

1/4 cup Stevia Base (see page 72)

6 tablespoons cream

2 tablespoons coconut palm sugar

1/4 teaspoon vanilla extract

1   In a saucepan on the lowest heat possible, stir together the oil and cocoa.
2   Add all of the remaining ingredients and whisk until smooth, about 1 minute. As soon as the center of the pan boils, turn off the heat.
3   Remove the sauce from the pan and pour into a bowl to let cool.

CARAMEL SAUCE

This recipe is perfect as an ice cream topping and can also be used for making caramel popcorn. One of my favorite ways to use this sauce is as a dip for slices of freshly picked red or green apples.

MAKES 1 1/2 CUPS CARAMEL SAUCE

4 tablespoons butter

1/4 cup coconut palm sugar

1 tablespoon whey isolate powder

1 cup Stevia Base (see page 72)

1 1/2 teaspoons vanilla extract

Pinch of salt

1   In a heavy-bottom saucepan, combine all the ingredients together over low heat, whisking until smooth.

2   Increase heat to medium-low and bring the mixture to a boil, stirring constantly (about 1 minute). When a full boil begins, stir the mixture slowly for 2 minutes.

3   Remove from heat and cool.

SWEETENED WHIPPED CREAM

Whipped cream is delicious on so many different things! So what makes this sweetened whipped cream healthy? The powdered sugar substitute gives the whipped cream just enough sweetness while keeping the texture fine and fluffy, all in a way that your body can process easily and without undue stress.

MAKES 1/2 CUP WHIPPED CREAM

1/2 cup whipping cream

1 tablespoon Sweet & Healthy Powdered Sugar Substitute (see page 77)

1   Whip the cream with an electric hand mixer until the cream forms hard peaks.
2   Add and mix the powdered sugar substitute into the whipped cream. Increase the amount of Powdered Sugar Substitute to taste.
3   Use immediately, or refrigerate for up to 2 days.

PERFECT SUGAR-FREE JAM (WITH OR WITHOUT SEEDS)

Fruit and berries are healthy, whole foods. There is no caloric sugar in this recipe, with the traditional sugar replaced by stevia (zero calories) and fruit puree. Best of all, this jam tastes like the fruit you make it from instead of cloying sugar.

MAKES 2 CUPS

12 ounces berries or stone fruit, fresh or frozen

1 cup water

1/2 cup Stevia Base (see page 72)

1 1/2 tablespoons Ball RealFruit Low or No-Sugar Needed Pectin

1   Combine all ingredients in a large heavy-bottom pot over medium heat. Do not use more than medium heat, as the jam can scald. While the water warms, mash the berries or fruit with a potato masher.

2   The mixture will slowly come to a boil (about 5 minutes if using frozen berries or fruit and less if using fresh berries or fruit). Whisk the mixture regularly as it comes to a boil.

3   When the mixture comes to a full rolling boil, whisk constantly for 1 minute. After 1 minute, turn off the heat.

4   If you are using berries and you don't want to remove any seeds, pour the jam into a bowl and let it cool to room temperature. Serve immediately, or for thicker jam, refrigerate for at least 1 hour, or freeze for storage.

5   For seedless berry jam, place a metal mesh sieve on a large bowl and pour the hot jam mixture through the sieve. Using a silicone spatula, press the jam through the sieve until only seeds remain. Scraping the bottom of the sieve is not recommended, as small seeds may come through. Allow the jam to cool to room temperature. The jam can be served immediately, or for thicker jam, refrigerate for at least an hour, or freeze for storage.

6   Find water-bathing directions on the pectin bottle, including the addition of lemon juice to certain kinds of fruit.

Some frozen fruits, especially inexpensive brands, contain a lot of ice. The additional liquid from the ice may prevent the pectin from setting in this recipe. Remove any excess ice from the frozen fruit before starting this recipe, or consider purchasing higher-quality frozen fruit.

If you are using stone fruit, remove the stones and skin and chop the fruit before beginning this recipe. Fruit skin is most easily removed by scalding the whole fruit in boiling water for a few seconds. Ladle out the scalded fruit and immediately plunge it into a bowl of ice water until cool enough to handle. The skin can then be pulled easily off the fruit.

MAPLE PANCAKE SYRUP

Saturday morning breakfast wouldn't be the same without syrupy deliciousness. Here is an incredible option to replace traditional sugary syrup. This recipe uses powdered sugar substitute, which won't spike your body's glycemic load, because it has a balance of sweetness and protein. With this syrup, you can enjoy pancakes and waffles covered in delicious maple sweetness.

MAKES 1/2 CUP SYRUP

1/2 cup water

3 tablespoons Sweet & Healthy Powdered
　Sugar Substitute (see page 77)

3 drops maple extract

1　Stir ingredients together in a saucepan.
2　On medium heat, bring the mixture to a boil and boil for 1 minute.
3　Serve warm.

MAPLE FRUIT PUREE PANCAKE SYRUP

This variation on traditional maple syrup is a popular choice at our house. It is rich and flavorful, perfect for a Saturday morning breakfast with the family.

MAKES 3/4 CUP SYRUP

1/4 cup warm water

1 tablespoon Sweet & Healthy Powdered
　Sugar Substitute (see page 77)

1/2 cup Stevia Base (see page 72)

3 drops maple extract

1　Whisk all ingredients together in a heavy-bottom saucepan over low heat. (Higher heat will scald the mixture.)
2　Bring the mixture to a boil. Boil for 1 minute.
3　Serve warm.

BERRY PASTRY GEL
WITHOUT SEEDS

This pastry gel is practically sugar-free compared to any other recipe like it, yet sweet and full of flavor thanks to the stevia and coconut palm sugar. The berries are a healthy, whole food. The flavor is tart, sweet, and refreshing.

MAKES 3 CUPS PASTRY GEL

2 cups cold water

1 packet Knox unflavored gelatin powder

1/4 cup coconut palm sugar, birch sugar, or Sweet & Healthy Powdered Sugar Substitute (see page 77)

1/4 teaspoon powdered stevia extract, 90 percent strength

12 ounces tart berries (raspberries, blackberries, boysenberries, or a mix of these), fresh or frozen

1   Put the cold water into a large, heavy-bottom saucepan. Whisk in the gelatin powder.
2   Whisk in the sugar and stevia extract.
3   Stir in the fresh or frozen berries and slowly bring the mixture to a boil on medium heat, stirring regularly (about 4–5 minutes if using frozen berries, less if using fresh berries). Avoid cooking on high heat, which will scald the mixture.
4   When the center of the pan begins to boil, turn off the heat. Do not allow the mixture to cool. Place a metal mesh sieve over a large glass or metal bowl. Using a silicone spatula, press the hot mixture through the sieve to strain out any seeds. Press thoroughly to get the most gel.
5   Discard the seeds. Scrape any gel clinging to the bottom of the sieve into the bowl, then pour the seedless gel back into the saucepan.
6   Bring the seedless mixture to a boil on medium heat again. When the center of the pan begins to boil, set a timer for 1 minute. After 1 minute, turn off the heat.
7   Pour the mixture into a glass or metal bowl and allow it to cool at room temperature for 1 hour.
8   After 1 hour, put the bowl into the fridge for at least 4 hours or overnight to form a gel.
9   Serve chilled.

WITH SEEDS

Like the seedless version, this pastry gel is practically sugar-free yet sweet and full of flavor thanks to the stevia, coconut palm sugar, and berries, and the flavor is tart, sweet, and refreshing. The advantage of this version is that, if you don't mind the seeds, the recipe takes half the time of the seedless version.

MAKES 3 CUPS PASTRY GEL

2 cups cold water

1 packet Knox unflavored gelatin powder

1/4 cup coconut palm sugar, birch sugar, or Sweet & Healthy Powdered Sugar Substitute (see page 77)

1/4 teaspoon powdered stevia extract, 90 percent strength

12 ounces tart berries (raspberries, blackberries, boysenberries, or a mix of these), fresh or frozen

1   Put the cold water into a large, heavy-bottom saucepan. Whisk in the gelatin powder.

2   Whisk in the palm sugar and stevia extract.

3   Stir in the fresh or frozen berries and slowly bring the mixture to a boil on medium heat, stirring regularly (about 4–5 minutes if using frozen berries, less if using fresh berries). Avoid cooking on high heat, which will scald the mixture.

4   When the center of the pan begins to boil, set a timer for 1 minute. After 1 minute, turn off the heat.

5   Pour the mixture into a glass or metal bowl and allow to cool at room temperature for 1 hour. After 1 hour, put the bowl into the fridge for at least 4 hours or overnight to form a gel.

6   Serve chilled.

GELATIN DESSERT

I grew up with and love gelatin treats, but the sugar in most mixes overwhelms the body. This alternative preserves the fun and flavor without the sugar.

MAKES 6 SERVINGS OF GELATIN

2 cups cold water

1 packet Knox unflavored gelatin powder

1 packet unsweetened Kool-Aid mix, in the flavor of your choice

1 measured pinch* of powdered stevia extract, 90 percent

1 tablespoon Sweet & Healthy Powdered Sugar Substitute (see page 77)

1 additional cup cold water

*A measured pinch is 1/16 of a teaspoon. Measuring spoon sets that include this size are available at cooking stores and Amazon.com.

1   In a small saucepan, whisk together all ingredients except the final cup of water.
2   On medium heat, slowly bring the mixture to a boil. Boil for 1 minute, then turn off the heat.
3   Pour the additional cup of cold water into a medium bowl. Pour in the hot liquid mixture and whisk the mixture and water together. Place the mixture into the fridge to chill and set up for at least 2 hours or overnight.
4   Serve chilled.

JIGGLY GELATIN TREATS

Gelatin desserts in little jiggly shapes give us a childlike whimsy, and this treat preserves the amazing taste and whimsy even as the stevia extract helps the body maintain a flattened glycemic load.

MAKES 6 GELATIN SERVINGS

2 cups warm water

1 unsweetened Kool-Aid packet, in the flavor of your choice

3 measured pinches* of powdered stevia extract, 90 percent strength

2 teaspoons Sweet & Healthy Powdered Sugar Substitute (see page 77)

2 packets Knox unflavored gelatin powder, or equivalent

*A measured pinch is 1/16 of a teaspoon. Measuring spoon sets that include this size are available at cooking stores and Amazon.com.

1 Whisk all ingredients together in a pan until completely incorporated.

2 Taste for sweetness. If you want the mixture sweeter, add tiny amounts of stevia powder to taste.

3 Bring to a full boil and boil for 1 minute, stirring occasionally.

4 Allow the mixture to rest until it stops steaming. To make jiggly treats, place a silicone candy mold on a plate (do not use a plastic mold). Carefully pour the hot liquid into the mold cavities until full, allowing any extra to spill onto the plate below.

5 Use a butter knife or spatula to level off the liquid on top of the mold. Move the plate holding the mold to the fridge. Allow to cool completely and set up for at least 2 hours or overnight.

6 When the candies are completely chilled and firm, pop them out of the mold cavities and serve cold.

> JIGGLE SQUARES OPTION: Pour the hot liquid mixture into an 8x8-inch baking dish. Transfer the dish to the fridge. Allow to cool completely and set up for at least 2 hours or overnight. When the gelatin is completely chilled and firm, cut into squares and serve cold.

COOKIES & BROWNIES

PUMPKIN CHOCOLATE CHIP COOKIES

The stevia-and-fruit puree used in this recipe significantly reduces the sugar and oil in these cookies, leaving them tasty and healthy. Cinnamon and pineapple have their own health benefits, including anti-inflammatory properties. And pumpkin puree is a whole food, perfectly ready for your body's use. Altogether, this recipe has a far lower glycemic index than traditional pumpkin chocolate chip cookies, as well as fewer calories and far more prebiotic fiber, protein, and nutrition.

MAKES APPROXIMATELY 3 DOZEN COOKIES; RECIPE CAN BE DOUBLED

1 cup pumpkin puree

1 1/2 cups Stevia Base (see page 72)

1/4 cup olive oil

1 egg

1/4 cup coconut palm sugar

1 cup whole wheat pastry flour

3/4 cup almond meal flour

1/3 cup protein powder (whey, hemp, or vegetable, as desired)

1 3/4 teaspoons baking powder

2 teaspoons cinnamon

1/2 teaspoon salt

1/2 teaspoon vanilla extract

1 cup chocolate chips

1   Preheat oven to 350 degrees.

2   In a large bowl, combine all ingredients using a handheld electric mixer.

3   Scoop mixture into balls and place on a cookie sheet lined with parchment paper or a silicone baking liner.

4   Bake the cookies for 12–13 minutes. Do not overbake, or the cookies will be dry instead of moist.

5   Allow the cookies to cool on the cookie sheet (they will be too delicate to move until they are cooled).

This recipe can be halved if you use a small egg.

PEANUT M&MS COOKIES

Believe it or not, glycemic load tests have shown over and over that Peanut M&Ms are probably the healthiest mass-produced candy on the planet (when eaten in moderation, as always) because the whole peanuts in them provide protein, which significantly drops their glycemic load on the body. All of the balanced ingredients make this recipe a great alternative to traditional candy or chocolate chip cookies.

MAKES A BAKER'S DOZEN (13) COOKIES; RECIPE CAN BE DOUBLED

1/2 cup Stevia Base (see page 72)

1/4 cup coconut palm sugar

1 measured pinch* powdered stevia leaf

1/2 cup almond meal flour

1/2 cup whole wheat pastry flour

Pinch of salt

1/2 teaspoon baking soda

1/3 cup butter, room temperature

1/4 teaspoon vanilla extract

1 cup Peanut M&Ms, Peanut Butter M&Ms, or Reese's Pieces

A measured pinch is 1/16 of a teaspoon. Measuring spoon sets that include this size are available at cooking stores and Amazon.com.

1 Preheat oven to 350 degrees.
2 Stir together the Stevia Base, coconut palm sugar, and powdered stevia leaf. The mixture will turn green (because of the natural chlorophyll in the stevia leaves), but don't worry—this green color will not be present in the final product.
3 Combine the remaining dry ingredients except the candy pieces in a bowl.
4 Add the butter and vanilla to the mixture, blending until just smooth. If using a stand mixer, use only the lowest setting. Do not overwork the ingredients, or the cookies will be tough.
5 Stir in the candy pieces until just coated with batter. Using a #40 scoop, scoop balls of dough and place on a cookie sheet lined with parchment paper or a silicone baking mat.
6 Bake the cookies for 13–14 minutes. Overbaking will cause the cookies to be dry.

When the cookies are baked, remove the cookie sheet from the oven but do not remove the cookies from the sheet. Because these cookies will be delicate, allow them to cool on the cookie sheet, not on a cookie rack.

NO-BAKE CHOCOLATE OATMEAL DROP COOKIES

This tasty alternative has low sugar, oil, salt, and butter because of the stevia-and-fruit puree and coconut palm sugar. These cookies are light, fluffy, and delicious. This is a popular recipe at our house, and, I confess that sometimes I eat just this for dinner when I'm home all alone.

MAKES 1 DOZEN COOKIES

4 tablespoons butter

2/3 cup Stevia Base (see page 72)

1/3 cup milk (or evaporated milk, which makes a creamier cookie)

2 tablespoons coconut palm sugar

1/4 cup Sweet & Healthy Powdered Sugar Substitute (see page 77)

2 1/2 tablespoons unsweetened cocoa powder

1/4 teaspoon salt

1 teaspoon vanilla extract

1 3/4 cups regular oats

1   In a heavy-bottom saucepan over low heat, whisk together all the ingredients except the oats until smooth. Bring to a low boil and boil for 1 minute.

2   Stir in the oats and immediately turn off the heat. Continue to stir until the oats are soft, about 30 seconds.

3   Using a small cookie scoop, scoop mixture into balls and place on wax paper, parchment paper, or a silicone baking liner. Let cookies cool for a couple of minutes before serving.

> I know some people feel butter should be avoided, but I'm not one of them (as long as butter is used in moderation). I have a problem with laboratory-created, processed butter substitutes, which I believe are supremely unhealthy. Butter is real food with real nutrients. Besides, no one on earth ate more butter than the high priestess of cookery, Julia Child, and she lived to be 91 years old!

PEANUT BUTTER CHOCOLATE CHIP COOKIES

This recipe is healthful because of several key ingredients. Peanut butter significantly lowers the glycemic load while being protein rich. Chickpea flour and almond flour are also protein rich. The stevia-and-fruit puree cuts down the sugar and butter, and there is little salt; coconut palm sugar offers more nutrients and a lower glycemic load; together, they taste incredible!

MAKES 1 DOZEN COOKIES

1/2 cup chickpea flour (or whole wheat pastry flour)

1/2 cup almond meal flour

3/4 teaspoon baking powder

1/2 cup coconut palm sugar

Pinch of salt (if your peanut butter doesn't already contain salt)

3 tablespoons Sweet & Healthy Powdered Sugar Substitute (see page 77)

1/4 cup Stevia Base (see page 72)

1/2 cup natural peanut butter

2 teaspoons vanilla extract

1/2 cup chocolate chips

1/8 cup additional Stevia Base

1. Preheat oven to 350 degrees.
2. Whisk together the flours, baking powder, salt, and sugars.
3. Using an electric hand mixer on the lowest setting, gradually stir the 1/4 cup Stevia Base into the flour mix until a crumbly mixture forms. (This is essential for making the cookies light.)
4. Continuing with the electric hand mixer on the lowest setting, mix in the peanut butter and vanilla until the mixture is fully combined and crumbly.
5. Add in the chocolate chips and the additional 1/8 cup Stevia Base. Mix on the lowest setting until just incorporated.
6. Scoop into balls and place on a cookie sheet lined with parchment paper or a silicone baking liner.
7. Bake the cookies for 12 minutes.

CHOCOLATE CHIP SNOW COOKIES

The original nonstevia version of this recipe is unhealthy with 1 1/2 cups of sugar. Concerned about health, more than a decade ago, we created a rule at our house that we could only make cookies when it was snowing. Even today, when the grandkids wake up to see snow on the ground, they run to the kitchen, saying, "It snowed! Can we make snow cookies?"

Making these cookies healthier was a slow process. Creating a stevia version that tasted as good as the original took many, many failed test batches, but I'm proud to say that not only is this guilt-free recipe delicious but also we no longer have to wait for snow at our house to make cookies!

MAKES 1 DOZEN COOKIES

1/2 cup whole wheat pastry flour

1/2 cup almond meal flour

Pinch of salt

1/4 cup coconut palm sugar

1/4 cup Stevia Base (see page 72)

1 teaspoon vanilla extract

3 tablespoons butter, room temperature

1 egg, separated, with the egg white beaten to soft peaks

1/4 teaspoon baking soda

1/2 cup chocolate chips

1 Preheat oven to 350 degrees.

2 Whisk all the dry ingredients except the baking soda together.

3 Add the Stevia Base*, vanilla, butter, and egg yolk into the flour mixture using a mixing spoon. If you use an electric handheld mixer, use the lowest setting. (Overworking the dough will cause the cookies to be chewy.)

4 Stir in the baking soda. Then stir in the soft peak egg white. Mix until just combined.

5 Stir in the chocolate chips.

6 Scoop into balls and place on a cookie sheet lined with parchment paper or a silicone baking liner. Bake the cookies for 10–11 minutes.

7 After the cookies are baked, allow them to rest on the cookie sheet until cool enough to handle. The cookies will be fragile and should not be moved while they are hot or they will fall apart.

Be sure to put in the Stevia Base after mixing the dry ingredients, according to the recipe, or these cookies will have a cake texture, which I don't prefer.

BROWNIES

This healthy recipe uses birch sugar (xylitol), which does not interact at all with the body's glycemic load, and coconut palm sugar, which has essentially the same amount of calories as refined white sugar but half the glycemic load and far more nutrients.

MAKES 16 2-INCH BROWNIES

4 tablespoons butter, melted

1/2 cup Stevia Base (see page 72)

1/2 cup coconut palm sugar

2 eggs

1 1/2 teaspoons vanilla extract

3 tablespoons unsweetened cocoa powder

1/4 cup birch sugar

1/3 cup almond meal flour

1/3 cup whole wheat pastry flour

3 tablespoons Sweet & Healthy Powdered Sugar Substitute (see page 77; I use half whey and half hemp protein in this recipe)

1/2 cup chocolate chips (optional)

Pinch of salt

1 Preheat oven to 350 degrees.
2 Stir all ingredients together, by hand or on the lowest setting of an electric hand mixer, until incorporated.
3 Pour the mixture into an ungreased 8x8-inch baking dish. Bake the brownies for 30 minutes.
4 Let the brownies cool, then cut and serve.

This recipe, without baking soda, makes a traditionally chewy brownie. If you want your brownies to have a more cake-like texture, put in a pinch of baking soda—but no more than a pinch, or they will be too cakey.

BLONDIES
(BLOND BROWNIES)

The whole wheat pastry flour used in this recipe has a much lower glycemic load and far more nutrition than white flour. Almond flour and whey powder are both protein rich, which helps flatten the glycemic load and add real nutrition—not to mention the lack of sugar and minimal butter, all of which make this a delicious, nutritious treat.

MAKES 16 2-INCH BLONDIES

4 tablespoons butter, melted

1/2 cup Stevia Base (see page 72)

1/4 cup coconut palm sugar

2 eggs

1 1/2 teaspoons vanilla extract

1/3 cup Sweet & Healthy Powdered Sugar
Substitute (see page 77)

1/3 cup almond meal flour

1/3 cup whole wheat pastry flour

2 tablespoons whey isolate protein powder

1/2 cup semisweet chocolate chips

Pinch of salt

1   Preheat oven to 350 degrees.
2   Stir all ingredients together, by hand or with an electric hand mixer on the lowest setting, until incorporated.
3   Pour the mixture into an ungreased 8x8-inch baking dish. Bake the brownies for 30 minutes.
4   Let the brownies cool, then cut and serve.

CAKES

Why are these recipes healthy? In the recipes for each of these cakes, I recommend using whole wheat pastry flour because it has a much lower glycemic load and far more nutrition than white flour. Also, while olive oil is considered a healthy oil, in these recipes I keep it to a minimum to reduce calories. Altogether, these cakes have a far lower glycemic index than traditional cake as well as fewer calories and far more protein, nutrition, and prebiotic fiber.

VANILLA CONTROVERSY CAKE

I call this "controversy cake" because health advocates everywhere will be horrified that I included this recipe. But in my defense, I have worked hard to make this recipe far healthier than any boxed or bakery cake. This is the only recipe in this cookbook that uses white flour (in this case, specialty cake flour). All grocery store cakes and cake mixes are made with specialty cake flour, available on the baking aisle at your grocery store. Cake flour is even worse on the glycemic index than normal white flour because it is specifically formulated to be low in protein—which is why it fluffs up so nicely. However, this recipe also includes almond meal flour, which has six grams of protein in a quarter cup, and is high in fiber, which helps reduce the glycemic load of this cake, despite the cake flour.

MAKES 6 SERVINGS

1 cup almond meal flour

1 cup cake flour

1/3 cup Sweet & Healthy Powdered Sugar Substitute (see page 77)

1/2 teaspoon baking powder

1/4 teaspoon baking soda

1/4 cup olive oil or 1/4 cup melted coconut oil plus 2 tablespoons cake flour

1 cup Stevia Base (see page 72)

1 egg, separated

1 1/2 tablespoons butter, melted

1 teaspoon vanilla extract

FLAVOR VARIATIONS:

For chocolate cake: add 3 tablespoons unsweetened cocoa powder and 1 tablespoon birch sugar (xylitol)

For dark chocolate cake: add 4 1/2 tablespoons unsweetened cocoa powder and 1 tablespoon birch sugar (xylitol)

For yellow cake: add 1 egg yolk

For butter cake: add 1 egg yolk and 1/4 teaspoon butter extract

For lemon cake: add 1 egg yolk and juice and zest of 1 lemon or 1/4 teaspoon lemon extract

1   Preheat oven to 350 degrees.
2   Whisk together the dry ingredients.

I don't mind the Cake Without Controversy recipe in this book, but years ago, when I started my journey toward health, I would have hated that cake just because it is dense rather than fluffy. And I will admit that I would never take Cake Without Controversy to a neighborhood or church gathering, work party, or any special occasion because people would turn up their noses; they would see it as too dense. They would not be interested in its health benefits, and I probably wouldn't get invited to many parties. But this Controversy Cake recipe is much healthier than traditional cake, and I promise you that no one would turn up their nose to it at a party; they likely would never suspect that it is healthier than traditional cakes. In the end, the choice is yours: cake with controversy or without. I include them both so that there will be cake for everyone, however far we are along the path to better health.

3   Whisk in the remaining ingredients, except the egg white, until just incorporated, taking care not to overwork the batter (which can result in dense cake).

4   In a separate bowl, beat the egg white until they form soft peaks. Using a spatula, fold the beaten egg white into the batter.

5   Pour the batter into a greased and floured 8x8-inch pan. Cover the pan with aluminum foil. (This reflects some of the top heat, helping to keep the top of the cake from browning too much, which will result in a flatter, denser cake.)

6   Bake the cake for approximately 35–38 minutes or until the tip of a knife inserted into the center of the cake comes out clean.

7   Cool completely in the pan before serving.

VANILLA CAKE WITHOUT CONTROVERSY

This cake will not be as fluffy as store-bought cakes because it does not use cake flour, which has little protein. Instead, this cake uses whole wheat pastry flour with lots of protein, though it makes the cake more dense. For truly fluffy cake, follow the recipe for Vanilla Controversy Cake.

MAKES 6 SERVINGS

3/4 cup whey protein powder

3/4 cup whole wheat pastry flour

1/2 teaspoon baking powder

1/4 teaspoon baking soda

1/3 cup Sweet & Healthy Powdered Sugar Substitute (see page 77)

3/4 cup Stevia Base (see page 72)

1/4 cup olive oil or 1/4 cup melted coconut oil plus 2 tablespoons wheat pastry flour

1 1/2 tablespoons butter, melted

1/3 cup milk

1 teaspoon vanilla extract

2 egg whites, beaten to soft peaks

FLAVOR VARIATIONS:

For chocolate cake: add 3 tablespoons unsweetened cocoa powder

For dark chocolate cake: add 4 1/2 tablespoons unsweetened cocoa powder

For yellow cake: add 1 egg yolk

For butter cake: add 1 egg yolk and 1/4 teaspoon butter extract

1   Preheat oven to 350 degrees.
2   Whisk together the dry ingredients.
3   Whisk in the remaining ingredients except the egg whites until just incorporated, taking care not to overwork the batter (which can result in dense cake).
4   With a spatula, fold the beaten egg whites into the batter.
5   Pour the batter into a greased and floured 8x8-inch pan. Cover the pan with aluminum foil. (This reflects some of the top heat, helping to keep the top of the cake from browning too much, which will result in a flatter, denser cake.)
6   Bake the cake for approximately 35–38 minutes or until the tip of a knife inserted into the center of the cake comes out clean.
7   Cool completely in the pan before serving.

CHOCOLATE MOUSSE REFRIGERATOR CAKE

For those special occasions when rich, creamy chocolate is a must, this Chocolate Mousse Refrigerator Cake fits the bill! Not only is it healthier than traditional cake recipes, it is rich and full of the nutrition that your body craves without sacrificing your indulgent sweet tooth.

MAKES 6 SERVINGS

1 Chocolate Controversy Cake or Chocolate Without Controversy, baked and cooled (see page 114 and page 117)

1/4 cup half-and-half or evaporated milk

1 cup Rich Chocolate Frosting (see page 83)

1/2 cup Sweetened Whipped Cream (see page 89)

1   Remove the 8x8-inch chocolate cake from the cake pan, cut it in half horizontally, trim as desired, and center one half on a cake plate to serve as the bottom layer of the cake. Set the other half aside.

2   Puncture the entire center of the bottom layer of cake with a fork, leaving 1 inch around the outside of the cake untouched.

3   Pour the half-and-half or evaporated milk over the bottom cake layer, particularly toward the center of the cake and over the punctures.

4   Frost the bottom layer with 1/3 of the frosting.

5   Using 1/3 of the whipped cream, frost over the chocolate frosting.

6   Place the top layer of cake over the frosting and cream on the bottom layer. Using 1/2 of the remaining frosting, frost the top layer of cake.

7   Add the remaining frosting to the remaining whipped cream. Mix until smooth with an electric hand mixer. Use 1/2 of the resulting mousse to crumb coat* the entire cake.

8   Use the remaining 1/2 of the mousse to frost the entire cake.

9   Refrigerate and serve.

*A crumb coat is a light layer of frosting over a cake that prevents crumbs from getting into the final coat of frosting.

CARAMEL LECHE CAKE
TOPPED WITH FRESH FRUIT

Caramel leche cake is one for those with a sweet tooth. So why is this recipe healthy? The cake recipe is already healthier than traditional cake recipes, but with stevia-sweetened whipped cream, stevia caramel frosting, and fresh fruit, this cake is creamy, moist, and delicious without sacrificing nutritional value.

MAKES 6 SERVINGS

1 Vanilla Controversy Cake or Without Controversy (see page 114 or page 117)

1/4 cup half-and-half or evaporated milk

1 1/2 cups Caramel Frosting (see page 85)

1/2 cup Sweetened Whipped Cream (see page 89)

4 cups of fresh fruit (kiwi, grapes, strawberries, blackberries, blueberries, peaches, nectarines, or plums)

1   Remove the 8x8-inch cake from the cake pan, cut it in half horizontally, trim as desired, and center one half on a cake plate to serve as the bottom cake layer. Set the other half aside.

2   Puncture the entire center of the bottom layer of cake with a fork, leaving 1 inch around the outside of the cake untouched.

3   Pour 1/2 of the half-and-half or evaporated milk over the bottom cake layer.

4   Frost the cake layer with 1/2 of the frosting.

5   Cover the frosting with 1/3 of the whipped cream.

6   Place about 2 cups of the fruit on top of the whipped cream.

7   Place the second layer of cake over the whipped cream and fruit. Puncture the top layer of cake with a fork, leaving 1 inch around the outside of the cake untouched. Pour on the remaining half-and-half or evaporated milk.

8   Repeat Steps 4 and 5 on the top layer.

9   Use the remaining whipped cream to frost the entire cake.

10 Decorate the top of the cake with the remaining fruit.

11 Serve immediately, or refrigerate for up to 1 day.

RASPBERRY CHOCOLATE PUDDING CAKE

The cake used in this recipe is already healthier than traditional cakes, but by using the recipes for raspberry jam and chocolate pudding from this book, this cake has a better balance of fiber, protein, and natural sweetness. The glycemic load on the body is low, and the flavor profile is high.

MAKES 6 SERVINGS

1 Vanilla Cake Without Controversy (see page 117)

1 cup Perfect Sugar-Free Jam, With or Without Seeds, prepared with raspberries (see page 90)

1 cup Chocolate Pudding (see page 127)

1/4 cup half-and-half or evaporated milk

1/2 cup Sweetened Whipped Cream (see page 89)

1   Remove the cooled vanilla cake from the cake pan, cut it in half horizontally, trim as desired, and center one half on a cake plate to serve as the bottom layer of the cake. Set the other half aside.

2   Puncture the entire center of the bottom layer of cake with a fork, leaving 1 inch around the outside of the cake untouched.

3   Pour 1/2 of the half-and-half or evaporated milk over the bottom layer of cake, especially toward the center and over the punctures.

4   Frost the top of this layer thickly with 1/2 of the jam.

5   Frost thickly over the jam with 1/2 of the pudding.

6   Place the second cake layer on top of the jam and pudding. Puncture the entire center of this top layer of cake with a fork, leaving 1 inch around the outside of the cake untouched.

7   Repeat Steps 3, 4, and 5 on the top cake layer.

8   Using 1/2 of the whipped cream, carefully crumb coat* the entire cake with a light touch so as not to mix the pudding and whipped cream.

9   Use the remaining whipped cream to frost the entire cake.

10 Serve immediately, or refrigerate for up to 1 day.

*A crumb coat is a light layer of frosting over a cake that prevents crumbs (or, for this cake, the chocolate pudding) from getting into the final coat of frosting.

STRAWBERRY VANILLA CAKE OPTION: Use vanilla pudding and strawberry jam to make this cake.

RASPBERRY MARZIPAN CAKE

I love the flavor of raspberries, which are rich whole foods. This healthier cake recipe makes the whole cake easier on the body's glycemic load, and the cream sweetened with stevia and berries makes this cake rich, moist, and better for your body.

MAKES 6 SERVINGS

- 3 cups Berry Pastry Gel, With or Without Seeds, prepared with raspberries (see page 94)
- 1 Yellow Controversy Cake or Without Controversy Cake (see page 114 or page 117)
- 2 tablespoons cream
- 1/2 cup whipping cream
- 1 measured pinch* powdered stevia extract, 90 percent strength
- 12 ounces fresh or frozen raspberries
- 1 package marzipan
- 1 tablespoon cornstarch or arrowroot powder

*A measured pinch is 1/16 of a teaspoon. Measuring spoon sets that include this size are available at cooking stores and Amazon.com.

1   Cut the cooled cake in half horizontally. Set one half of the cake on a cake plate to serve as the bottom layer of the cake, and set the other half aside.

2   Using the tines of a fork, poke holes into the bottom layer of cake. Drizzle 2 tablespoons of cream over this layer.

3   Whip together the whipping cream and stevia extract to form soft peaks.

4   Pipe 1/2 of the pastry gel over the bottom cake layer. Top this with 6 ounces of the fresh or frozen raspberries. Then cover with 1/4 of the whipped cream mixture.

5   Place the remaining layer of cake on top of the bottom layer. Repeat Step 4.

6   Split the remaining whipping cream in half, using one part to crumb coat* the entire cake.

7   Use the remaining whipped cream to frost the entire cake. (It is important to cover the entire cake because any part of the cake that is not covered in whipped cream will show through the marzipan layer of the finished cake, giving the cake a blotchy and unprofessional appearance.)

8   Roll out the prepared marzipan on a flat surface, using a dusting of the cornstarch or arrowroot powder to keep the marzipan from adhering to the surface and roller. When rolled out large enough to cover the cake, drape the marzipan over the cake.

9   Roll and pinch the excess to form a piecrust-type border around the bottom of the cake, if desired, and trim any excess.

10 Serve chilled. (The flavor of this cake actually improves if refrigerated for a day—if you can wait that long to serve it!)

A crumb coat is a light layer of frosting over a cake that prevents crumbs from getting into the final coat of frosting.

CAKES

PIES

CARAMEL APPLE ICEBOX PIE

Apples are a whole food. And while the amount of cream used in this recipe is small, it provides calcium. Overall, this is delicious pie yet far healthier than anything else like it.

MAKES 6 SERVINGS

1 1/2 cups hot Caramel Sauce (see page 88)

3 clean, firm apples

1/2 cup whipping cream

1 measured pinch* powdered stevia extract, 90 percent strength

1 prepared piecrust or graham cracker crust (optional)

A measured pinch is 1/16 of a teaspoon. Measuring spoon sets that include this size are available at cooking stores and Amazon.com.

1 Pour hot caramel sauce into a 4-cup measuring cup.
2 Peel, remove core from, and dice apples one at a time, stirring the diced apple chunks into the hot caramel sauce until the sauce and apples together equal 3 cups. (This may not require all three apples, depending on the size of your apples.)
3 In a bowl, beat the whipped cream and stevia together until the cream forms and holds soft peaks.
4 With a spatula, fold the caramel-apple mix into the whipped cream. Fill the piecrust with the mixture and chill for 1 hour before serving.

CRUSTLESS OPTION: Portion the pie filling into individual dessert cups, chill for 1 hour, and serve.

SOFT SERVE OPTION: I like the apples in this recipe to be a little crunchy, but if you want them soft, after Step 2, warm the caramel-apple mix on the stove for two minutes on medium-low heat. Cool mixture completely before continuing to Step 3.

PUDDING

Stevia replaces most of the sugar found in the traditional version of this recipe, while the protein in the egg yolks flattens the slight glycemic load of the palm sugar.

MAKES 6 CUPS

1/4 cup coconut palm sugar

1/4 teaspoon powdered stevia extract, 90 percent strength

3 tablespoons cornstarch or arrowroot powder

Pinch of salt

2 cups milk

3 egg yolks

2 tablespoons Sweet & Healthy Powdered Sugar Substitute (see page 77)

2 tablespoons butter

1 teaspoon vanilla extract, or seeds scraped from inside 1 vanilla bean

FLAVOR OPTIONS:

For chocolate pudding: add 3 tablespoons unsweetened cocoa powder

For lemon pudding: add the juice and zest of 1 lemon

PIES

1   In a heavy-bottom saucepan, whisk all ingredients until incorporated. (This step must be done before ingredients are heated or the pudding will be lumpy.)
2   Place the pan on the stove on medium heat. Whisk the mixture while bringing to a boil.
3   As soon as the mixture begins to boil, turn the heat to low. Whisk constantly at a slow boil for 2 minutes.
4   Remove pan from heat. Spoon the pudding into a bowl and allow the pudding to rest on the counter until it stops steaming. Move to the fridge to cool and set.
5   Serve cold.

PIE OPTION: After the pudding has stopped steaming in Step 3, pour it into a baked piecrust and allow it to set up in the fridge. Serve chilled.

KEY LIME CHEESECAKE

The sugar in the traditional version of this recipe, usually contributed by sweetened condensed milk, has been replaced by pure fruit puree, with its healthy fiber, and a small amount of birch sugar, which does not stress the body's metabolism.

MAKES 6 SERVINGS

4 ounces cream cheese, softened

2 large eggs

1 can (15 ounces) evaporated milk

1/3 cup Stevia Base (see page 72)

1/3 cup key lime juice

Zest of 1 lime or 3 key limes

3 tablespoons whey protein powder

1/4 teaspoon salt

2 tablespoons Sweet & Healthy Powdered Sugar Substitute (see page 77)

1 prepared graham cracker piecrust

1   Preheat oven to 350 degrees.
2   In a large bowl, beat the cream cheese until fluffy using a handheld electric mixer.
3   Add all other filling ingredients and blend together until fairly smooth. (There will be some cream cheese lumps.)
4   Pour the filling into the piecrust. Bake for 20–25 minutes or just until the center is set.
5   Chill and serve.

GARNISH OPTION: When cooled, the top of the pie can be dusted with 2 teaspoons of Sweet & Healthy Powdered Sugar Substitute.

CRUSTLESS OPTION: The crust adds about 110 calories per serving, and in my experience, most people don't like the crust enough to eat it. Save the calories by going crustless. Just bake the pie filling in a greased and floured 8x8-inch baking dish or 9-inch pie plate.

LEMON CUSTARD PUDDING

This Lemon Custard is delightful and satisfying. It's flavor is bolstered by the Stevia Base and fresh lemon juice, and the whey powder in the sugar substitute is protein rich, adding real nutrition.

MAKES 6 SERVINGS

2 tablespoons butter, melted

1/3 cup Sweet & Healthy Powdered Sugar Substitute (see page 77)

3/4 cup Stevia Base (see page 72)

1/2 cup milk

1/4 teaspoon vanilla extract

Pinch of salt

Juice and zest of 2 lemons

2 tablespoons cornstarch

3 eggs, beaten

1   In a heavy-bottom saucepan, whisk all the ingredients except the eggs until incorporated.
2   Warm the pan on medium heat. Whisk the mixture while bringing to a boil. As soon as the mixture begins to boil, turn the stove to low heat. Whisk constantly at a slow boil for two minutes.
3   Remove the pan from heat and slowly whisk in the eggs.
4   Put the pudding mix into a bowl and let cool in the fridge.
5   Serve cold.

RASPBERRY VALENTINE PIE

The amount of cream (and therefore calories) used in this recipe is quite small compared to other cream pies. There is no added sugar beyond the very small amount in the pastry gel recipe. Berries are a whole food. For an even healthier adaptation, the crustless option for this pie saves about 110 calories per serving. Altogether, this pie is almost totally a whole food, with an addicting flavor that I crave.

MAKES 6 SERVINGS

1/2 cup whipping cream

1/4 teaspoon powdered stevia extract, 90 percent strength

3 cups Berry Pastry Gel (With or Without Seeds), prepared with raspberries and chilled (see page 94)

12 ounces raspberries, frozen or fresh

1 store-bought graham cracker piecrust

1   Using an electric hand mixer, whip the cream and stevia together to form soft peaks.
2   Stir together the whipping cream, stevia extract, Berry Pastry Gel, and raspberries until it is well blended. Fill the crust with the pie filling, chill, and serve.
3   To make a layered pie, put the chilled raspberry pastry gel into a pastry bag, or a plastic food storage bag with one bottom corner cut off, to form a pastry piping bag. Pipe a swirl of the gel onto the bottom of the piecrust. Spread the gel with a spatula to coat the piecrust evenly.
4   Using a spatula, fold 3/4 of the remaining raspberry pastry gel and 6 ounces of the raspberries into the whipped cream. Use the mixture to fill the piecrust.
5   Pipe the remaining raspberry gel in a swirl or lattice over the top of the pie. Decorate with the remaining raspberries.
6   Serve chilled.

I must tell you that this recipe is my favorite ever. When I created this recipe, I wanted to give myself some kind of genius award. I am a huge raspberry lover, though you can make this recipe with strawberries, boysenberries, or blackberries. This is a favorite at both Valentine's Day and Christmas, when I make this pie over and over again. (Truth be told, I make this pie all the time!)

BERRY PIE OPTION: Strawberries, blackberries, or a mix of your favorite berries can be used instead of raspberries both to make the Berry Pastry Gel called for in this recipe and as the berries in the pie. The berries can be fresh or frozen.

FRUIT PIE OPTION: Yellow peaches, nectarines, mangoes, or another favorite stone fruit can be used to make the Berry Pastry Gel and as the fruit in this recipe. Fresh white peaches are the author's favorite. The fruit can be fresh or frozen.

FROZEN PIE OPTION: This pie can be made ahead of time and frozen and served when partially thawed. This option is especially good on a hot summer day!

ICE CREAM PIE OPTION: To turn this recipe into an ice cream pie, substitute 1 1/2 cups ice cream (vanilla or a flavor compatible with your fruit or berries) for the whipped cream in this recipe. Prepare the pie, freeze, and serve.

TRIFLE OPTION: To make a trifle out of this recipe, break a graham cracker or shortbread crust into pieces and use them as a layer in the trifle.

PECAN PIE

Pecans are protein rich and help flatten the glycemic load. The coconut palm sugar adds a brown sugar flavor. Pecans and birch sugar together bring a caramel flavor and texture to this pie. Also, evaporated milk has far fewer calories and sugar than sweetened condensed milk. All in all, this pie is sweet, caramel-y, and rich while still being healthy—probably the healthiest pecan pie on the planet.

MAKES 6 SERVINGS

1/4 cup Stevia Base (see page 72)

2 eggs

1 teaspoon vanilla extract

1/4 cup evaporated milk

4 tablespoons melted butter

3/4 cup Sweet & Healthy Powdered Sugar Substitute (see page 77)

Pinch of salt

1/4 cup coconut palm sugar

5 ounces (1 1/4 cups) pecans

1 prepared piecrust

1   Preheat oven to 350 degrees.
2   Whisk together the wet ingredients, then add the Powdered Sugar Substitute, salt, and palm sugar.
3   Fold the pecans into the filling mixture. Pour the filling into the piecrust.
4   Bake for 30 minutes. Let cool, then serve.

SWEET, SAVORY & SALTY

PUMPKIN QUICK BREAD

Nothing tastes or smells more like autumn than fresh pumpkin bread, and this recipe is healthier than traditional pumpkin bread because it uses whole wheat pastry flour instead of white baking flour. This substitution increases the protein in the bread. Add to this the pumpkin puree and cinnamon, which have lots of nutrients, and you get a satisfying and delicious pastry for autumn.

MAKES 1 LOAF

1 cup whole wheat pastry flour

1 teaspoon baking powder

3/4 teaspoon salt

1/2 teaspoon cinnamon

1/4 teaspoon nutmeg

1/4 teaspoon ground ginger

1/8 teaspoon ground clove

1/3 cup coconut palm sugar

1/3 cup Sweet & Healthy Powdered Sugar Substitute (see page 77)

1 cup canned pumpkin puree

2 eggs

1/4 cup vegetable oil

3/4 cup Stevia Base (see page 72)

1 Preheat oven to 350 degrees.
2 Whisk together the dry ingredients.
3 Whisk in the wet ingredients until just incorporated. (Overworking the batter can result in a dense loaf.)
4 Pour the mixture into a greased and floured loaf pan. Bake for 55 minutes or until a knife inserted in the center of the loaf comes out clean.

STEVIA FRUIT DIP

Fruity desserts combine natural sweetness and nutrient-rich whole foods. This recipe combines sweet fruit with creamy stevia dip to make a great alternative to traditional fruit dip.

MAKES APPROXIMATELY 1 1/3 CUPS DIP

4 ounces cream cheese, softened

1/2 cup whipping cream, whipped to soft peaks

1/8 teaspoon powdered stevia extract, 90 percent strength

1 1/2 tablespoons Sweet & Healthy Powdered Sugar Substitute (see page 77)

1 tablespoon lime juice

Assorted fresh fruit of your choice, cut and peeled

1   In a large glass bowl, use an electric hand mixer to beat the cream cheese until smooth.

2   Add all remaining ingredients except the fruit pieces and beat the mixture on low until smooth. Chill and serve with the prepared fresh fruit for dipping.

FIDDLER'S BARBECUE SAUCE

This sauce is one of those rare recipes that gets better and better as it is slow-cooked. I like to call this "Fiddler's Sauce" because I know that everyone who uses this recipe will fiddle with it, as everyone does with barbecue sauces. And you *should* fiddle with it. My goal with this recipe is to give you a basic sauce that is healthy, and then you can tweak it with your favorite ingredients or to better match the situation—meatballs may want more tomato sauce and less fruit puree, while turkey may want a different kind of fruit puree and less tomato sauce, and fish will probably want no tomato sauce at all. So enjoy and have fun tinkering with this sauce while feeling good because you know it is far healthier than other barbecue sauces!

MAKES ABOUT 2 CUPS SAUCE

8 ounces tomato sauce or pureed fresh tomatoes

3/4 cup Stevia Base (see page 72)

1/4 cup water

1/4 cup coconut palm sugar

1 onion, chopped

3 tablespoons Worcestershire sauce

2 tablespoons prepared yellow mustard or powdered mustard

1/2 cup vinegar (white or flavor of your choice)

1   Whisk together all ingredients.
2   Pour over or use to baste or marinate meat. Cook as needed.

SAUCE VARIATIONS:

THICKER: forgo the water in the recipe
SWEETER: replace the water with additional Stevia Base
TANGIER: use balsamic vinegar, rice wine vinegar, or red wine vinegar
PORK: replace the tomato sauce with 1 part lime juice and 1 part mango or persimmon puree

FLAVOR VARIATIONS (AMOUNTS BY TASTE):

- Ground black pepper
- Ground white pepper
- Puree of orange, pomelo, mango, lime, etc.
- Fresh-crushed or roasted garlic, or garlic powder
- 2 tablespoons birch sugar (xylitol)
- Shallots
- Rosemary
- Winter savory
- Sweet mace
- Zest of lemon, lime, or pomelo

SWEET LEAF PIZZA SAUCE

Traditional pizza sauce has lots of sugar, but it doesn't need to! This pizza sauce is full of great flavor, balanced just right with a bit of stevia sweetness.

MAKES ENOUGH SAUCE FOR TWO LARGE PIZZAS

1 1/2 cups pureed fresh tomatoes

1/2 teaspoon oregano

1/2 teaspoon basil

1/4 teaspoon thyme

1/4 teaspoon sweet marjoram

1 clove of garlic, minced

1/4 teaspoon powdered stevia leaf

1 tablespoon extra-virgin olive oil

1 Stir all ingredients together in a saucepan.
2 Bring the mixture to boil over medium heat. Reduce the heat and simmer until the sauce reaches your desired thickness. Cool the sauce before using to top pizzas.

HOMEMADE VANILLA YOGURT

Yogurt is full of protein and calcium, but it is also traditionally full of sugar! This recipe balances nutritional value with great taste, leaving out the sugar and the guilt.

MAKES 1 CUP YOGURT

1 cup Viili Finnish Perpetual Probiotic Yogurt (starters available at SeedRenaissance.com), or 1 cup plain unsweetened store-bought yogurt

1 smidgen (half a pinch) of powdered stevia extract, 90 percent strength

4 drops vanilla extract

1   Stir all ingredients together until mixed.
2   Serve chilled.

STEVIA CARAMEL

Caramel is a great treat, and with this recipe you can enjoy it all the time, on popcorn or apple slices. This caramel cools thicker than the Caramel Sauce (see page 88) which makes it great for popcorn. The coconut palm sugar used has a rich taste similar to brown sugar but without the glycemic load on your body.

MAKES 1/2 CUP CARAMEL

3 tablespoons butter

3 tablespoons Stevia Base (see page 72)

2 tablespoons Sweet & Healthy Powdered
   Sugar Substitute (see page 77)

1 tablespoon coconut palm sugar

1/2 teaspoon vanilla extract

Pinch of salt (optional)

1   In a saucepan, melt the butter on low heat.

2   Leaving the heat on low, stir the remaining ingredients into the butter. Without increasing the heat, allow the mixture to come to a boil.

3   Boil for 2 minutes for soft caramel or 4 minutes for firmer caramel.

COCONUT OIL CARAMEL OPTION: Replace the butter in this recipe with coconut oil.

CARAMEL FLAVOR OPTIONS: I love to make this caramel with different citrus flavors, which make the caramel taste unbelievable. Try one of these:

- 3 tablespoons fresh-squeezed grapefruit juice and a pinch of grapefruit zest
- 1/4 cup orange juice and a pinch of orange zest
- 1/4 cup mulled orange juice and a pinch of orange zest
- 1/4 cup pomelo juice and a pinch of pomelo zest

CARAMEL POPCORN OPTION: Pop 1/4 cup popcorn kernels and drizzle caramel (regular or any of the flavor options) over the popcorn. Salt lightly, stir with a spatula, and serve as soon as the caramel is cool enough to eat safely.

CARAMEL CHOCOLATE CHIP BARS

SWEET, SAVORY & SALTY

On-the-go snacks that are healthy, filling, and tasty are hard to find. These Caramel Chocolate Chip Bars are a great solution because they are full of delicious protein, fiber, and sweetness.

MAKES 8 1-INCH BARS

3/4 cup Stevia Base (see page 72)

3/4 cup oats

1 egg

1/4 cup whole wheat pastry flour

1/2 cup almond meal flour

1/3 teaspoon vanilla extract

1/4 teaspoon baking soda

1/3 teaspoon baking powder

Pinch of salt

1 cup Stevia Caramel (see page 88)

3 tablespoons butter, melted

1/2 cup chocolate chips

1   Preheat oven to 350 degrees.
2   Stir together all ingredients except chocolate chips until just incorporated.
3   Line an 8x8-inch baking dish with aluminum foil. Spray the foil with cooking spray.
4   Pour the batter into the baking dish and spread it evenly over the foil.
5   Sprinkle the chocolate chips onto the batter.
6   Bake the mixture for 30 minutes.
7   Cut into bars and serve warm.

QUICK PEANUT BUTTER STEVIA SANDWICHES

In my house, we often seem to be looking for a quick lunch, especially for the younger grandkids. This recipe is the answer. The whole thing can be made and served in less than a minute, and there is absolutely nothing unhealthy about it.

MAKES 2 SANDWICHES

2 tablespoons peanut butter

3 tablespoons Stevia Base (see page 72)

4 slices of bread of your choice

1   Stir together the peanut butter and Stevia Base until completely mixed.
2   Spread the mixture onto the bread slices and serve. Do not use the Stevia Base as a layer (like jam) on the sandwich, because the base is bitter on its own.

Typical peanut butter sandwiches are slathered with sugary jams, jellies, or honey—all of which can spike the glycemic index and add calories. While it is true that peanut butter flattens the glycemic load of sugar, there is still no reason to use sugar if we don't have to, especially when you can replace the sugar with fruit, as this sandwich does. Putting the whole thing on wheat bread instead of white is healthier, too. Or, best yet, use natural yeast bread, which you can read about in *The Art of Baking with Natural Yeast*, a book I coauthored with Melissa Richardson.

DRINKS

BARCELO WATERMELON PUNCH

You may wonder, *Why not just blend up watermelon to make this punch? Why make it with stevia?* My answer: so you can eat your watermelon and drink it, too. It takes just a center-cut, one-inch-thick slice of watermelon to make a gallon of this punch, leaving the majority of your watermelon for eating. That is a win-win to me!

MAKES ABOUT 1 GALLON OF PUNCH

4 cups water

4 teaspoons powdered stevia extract, 90 percent strength

4 cups 1-inch watermelon chunks

2 cups ice

1   Combine 2 cups of the water in a blender with 2 teaspoons of the stevia. Add 2 cups of the watermelon chunks and blend until smooth. Pour the mixture into a pitcher.

2   Repeat Step 1. Because there is natural variation in watermelons, it is a good idea to taste the punch and add additional stevia to make it sweeter if needed.

3   Add ice to the punch, stir, and serve.

CHERRY LIME PUNCH

In this recipe, stevia replaces any sugar, and the fresh cherries are a great compliment to the lime juice.

MAKES ABOUT 1 GALLON OF PUNCH

3/4 gallon water

3/4 teaspoon powdered stevia extract, 90 percent strength

Juice of 4–5 limes

2 cups cherries, chopped and mashed

2 cups ice

1   Pour the water into a large pitcher. Stir in the stevia and lime juice.
2   Add the cherries and ice and stir briefly. Serve immediately.

SUMMER CITRUS PUNCH

Though this recipe has no sugar, it has a naturally sweet grapefruit flavor that makes it wonderfully refreshing. And there's no guilt and minimal glycemic load!

MAKES ABOUT 1 GALLON OF PUNCH

3/4 gallon water

Juice of 3 pink grapefruits, sieved to remove seeds and large pulp

3/4 teaspoon powdered stevia extract, 90 percent strength

4 cups ice

1   Stir the water, juice, and stevia in a pitcher.
2   Add the ice and stir briefly. Serve immediately.

HEALTHY PUNCH

Punch is a convenience drink, quick and easy to make, with flavors kids love. Making it with Kool-Aid and stevia instead of sugar protects the body's glycemic load. Some people may object to the artificial flavors in Kool-Aid, but in my opinion, Kool-Aid made with stevia is a far better option than any soda or energy drink.

MAKES 2 QUARTS

2 quarts water, or amount of water required per packet instructions

1 packet Kool-Aid powder (Peach-Mango, Pineapple, and Tropical Punch work best)

1/3 teaspoon powdered stevia extract, 90 percent strength

1   Pour the water into a pitcher. Mix the Kool-Aid powder and stevia into the water.
2   Taste a small amount and add more stevia in amounts the size of a pinhead to achieve desired sweetness.

Exceptionally fine powders sometimes have difficulty absorbing into water because of static electricity. The best way to mix stevia into Kool-Aid is to whisk the Kool-Aid and the stevia powders into 1 cup of hot tap water completely, then add the rest of the cold water and ice.

If you prefer a Kool-Aid flavor that is not listed above, use the same amount of stevia mixed with 1/4 cup Sweet & Healthy Powdered Sugar Substitute recipe (see page 77). Taste the mixture and add more powdered sugar substitute until the flavor suits your taste. While the powdered sugar substitute has one-third fewer calories than regular sugar, it does have calories. More importantly, however, it does not interact with the body's glycemic load, making it a much better option than refined sugar.

STEVIA LAVENDER CHAMOMILE TEA

This healthy tea is sweetened with stevia instead of sugar. This recipe is for chamomile and lavender because lavender is one of the best but least used culinary flavors, and both are naturally calming. However, this recipe is really just an example; I include it only to make the point that you can sweeten any tea, or any drink, without sugar when you use stevia. You can even use fresh green stevia leaves from your garden, like I do, if you have them. In summer, use this recipe as an iced tea or even a sun tea.

MAKES 1 SERVING

1/2 teaspoon dried chamomile, or 1 chamomile tea bag

1/2 teaspoon fresh or dried lavender flowers

1 measured pinch* powdered stevia extract, 90 percent strength

*A measured pinch is 1/16 of a teaspoon. Measuring spoon sets that include this size are available at cooking stores and Amazon.com.

1   Steep the chamomile and lavender in boiling water to make tea.
2   Remove the herbs by straining (or use a tea ball).
3   Stir in the stevia and enjoy.

HOT CHOCOLATE

It takes a lot of sugar to sweeten cocoa, which is naturally bitter. Here, stevia does the job in place of sugar, making hot chocolate with no guilt, no glycemic spike, and no sugar high followed by a sugar crash.

MAKES 6-8 SERVINGS

6–8 tablespoons Milk Chocolate Stevia
Sauce (see page 86)

6–8 cups milk

DRINKS

1   In a saucepan on the stove, warm 6-8 cups of milk (1 cup per serving).
2   Stir in 6–8 tablespoons of chocolate sauce into the milk (1 tablespoon per cup of milk). If you want a stronger or weaker chocolate flavor, adjust the amount of chocolate sauce according to your preference. Serve plain or with a dollop of Sweetened Whipped Cream (see page 89).

MULLED CHRISTMAS LEMONADE

Traditionally, there is no added sugar in mulled cider, but apple juice actually has a higher glycemic load than most soda, believe it or not. This recipe does away with the apple juice, replacing it with homemade lemonade. Mulling spices are naturally anti-inflammatory, soothing, and expectorant—in other words, the perfect winter drink.

MAKES 6-8 SERVINGS

3 cups water

1 teaspoon powdered stevia leaf

1 teaspoon mulling spice blend

Juice and zest of 1 lemon

1   Combine all ingredients in a saucepan. Bring to a boil and boil for 1 minute.
2   Strain through cheesecloth and serve hot or warm.

NUTRITIONAL AND MEDICINAL GREEN SMOOTHIES

Garden greens, fruits, and berries are filled with vital nutrition and critical prebiotic fiber. Fruits and berries naturally contain the simple sugars that your muscles, organs, and brain must have to function. Green smoothies provide all of this, and they are delicious, too (when prepared correctly).

MAKES 1 1/2 CUPS GREEN SMOOTHIE OR ONE SERVING

3/4 cup kefir or Viili Finnish Perpetual Probiotic Yogurt (starters available at SeedRenaissance.com)

1 handful of greens

3/4 teaspoon powdered stevia leaf, or 1 pinch powdered stevia extract, 90 percent strength

3/4 cup diced fruit or berries, fresh or frozen

1/2 teaspoon medicinal powdered or dried herbs, as desired (optional)

1   Combine all the ingredients in a blender, starting with the kefir or yogurt.
2   Pulse on a low gear until the greens are shredded. Then blend on a high gear until smooth.
3   Serve chilled.

The health benefits of properly prepared green smoothies cannot be overstated. For green smoothies to be truly powerful for the body, they should begin with a base of natural milk kefir or Finnish viili. These two fermented milk products have a huge influence on our health, and both have been used for thousands of years. Both are truly easy to make, and both are room-temperature starters. (Starters for both are available at SeedRenaissance.com, and once you have a starter, you can make yogurt and milk kefir for the rest of your life.)

Both contain a natural mix of beneficial probiotic bacteria and yeasts. Lactose intolerance is a problem for a growing number of people whose gut health has been compromised by the lack of a prebiotic and probiotic diet. Prebiotics like kefir and viili are composed of naturally occurring beneficial bacteria and yeasts that are critical to proper digestion in the gut. Prebiotics break down food, making it more bioavailable to the human digestive system. Without them, some of the nutrition we need passes through us instead of being taken up by the body, especially minerals and basic nutrients.

According to the *Handbook of Animal-Based Fermented Food and Beverage Technology, Second Edition*, both kefir and viili:

- when present in our gut, produce enzymes which hydrolyze the food we eat. *Hydrolysis* means that complex compounds are broken down so they are more easily used by the body.
- break down lactose and predigest milk proteins, so that instead of irritating the digestive tract, the lactose and proteins can be digested.
- due to the natural fermentation action, hydrolyze other milk proteins that cause milk allergies in some people, making them harmless (Rasic and Kurmann, 1978).
- increase the content of B vitamins (Oberman and Libudzisz, 1998).
- increase human absorption of the natural calcium in milk (Oberman and Libudzisz, 1998).
- increase human absorption of the natural iron in milk (Oberman and Libudzisz, 1998).
- inhibit the growth of pathogenic microorganisms in the human digestive tract. This means that the good bacteria and yeasts are protected and the bad bacteria and yeasts are controlled or destroyed. The competitive ability of both kefir and viili to inhibit had bacterial growth in the human gut has been shown in repeated scientific studies (Oberman and Libudzisz, 1998).
- "inhibit the action of some cancers" (Oberman and Libudzisz, 1998).
- decrease cholesterol levels in the blood (Oberman and Libudzisz, 1998, Nakajima et al., 1992, and Pigeon et al. 1992).
- boost and regulate the human immune system (Kitazawa et al., 1992).
- inhibit tumor growth in the human body (Chabot et al., 2001).
- allow beneficial bacteria to better adhere to and survive the human digestive tract, which allows for continuity of beneficial bacteria in the digestive tract (Ruas-Madiedo et al., 2006).

1. Y. H. Hui and E. Özgül Evranuz, *Handbook of Animal-Based Fermented Food and Beverage Technology, Second Edition* (Boca Raton, FL: CRC Press, 2012).

RECIPE INDEX

ABOUT THE AUTHOR

Caleb Warnock lives on the bench of the Rocky Mountains with his wife and family. He enjoys gardening, and he draws and paints when he is not writing, teaching, packing and shipping seeds, or creating new recipes. He can be found on Facebook or at CalebWarnock.blogspot.com. He sells pure, never-GMO, never-hybrid vegetable seeds (including some of the rarest seeds in the world) at SeedRenaissance.com. He is the bestselling author of eight nonfiction books and one fiction novel with recipes.

CALEB'S BOOKS

The Art of Baking With Natural Yeast: Breads, Pancakes, Waffles, Cinnamon Rolls & Muffins (coauthored by Melissa Richardson)
Most people don't know that yeast in the grocery store has been modified in a laboratory until it no longer digests the gluten naturally found in wheat. Natural yeast (also called *sourdough*, although it doesn't have to be sour) acts to prevent gluten intolerance, does not spike the glycemic index, controls allergies, and prevents heartburn.

Backyard Winter Gardening: Vegetables Fresh and Simple, In Any Climate, Without Artificial Heat or Electricity—The Way It's Been Done for 2,000 Years
Growing fresh winter vegetables is what fed our ancestors for centuries before the invention of the modern grocery store. This is the first vegetable-by-vegetable guide to fresh winter gardening published in the United States, and it includes carrots, onions, cantaloupes, beans, peas, lettuce, greens, and much more.

Forgotten Skills of Self-Sufficiency Used by the Mormon Pioneers
This book discusses backyard seed saving, the pioneer vegetable seed bank, an introduction to baking with natural yeast, cellaring without a root cellar, organic raised bed gardening, heirloom fruit trees, perennial flower gardens, recipes, and more.

Trouble's on the Menu: A Tippy Canoe Romp—With Recipes (coauthored by Betsy Schow)
After her estranged husband's unexpected death, Hallie goes to Tippy Canoe, Montana, to wrap up his estate. Her arrival begins awkwardly as she runs over the town gossip during a snowstorm. Fortunately, the single, attractive town mayor is willing to lend her a hand. But when life starts to spiral out of control, Hallie must decide whether he's worth sticking around for. (Caleb's favorite recipe: Hot Snow Chocolate.)

More Forgotten Skills of Self-Sufficiency

Bestselling author Caleb Warnock is back with a new collection of skills to help your family gain independence and self-reliance. Learn about self-seeding vegetables, collecting water from rain and snow, finding wild vegetables for everyday eating, and even making your own laundry soap. If you liked the first *Forgotten Skills* book, then you will love these additional techniques for becoming truly self-sufficient.

Forgotten Skills of Backyard Herbal Healing and Family Health (co-authored by Kirsten Skirvin)

Modern medicine can work wonders, but most of it has roots in the healing powers you can find in your own backyard. This informative book teaches you to harvest, dry, and store herbs that will keep you healthy. Discover how to use natural remedies safely, so you can nurture your family's wellness without leaving home.

Make Your Own Cheese: Self-Sufficient Recipes for Cheddar, Parmesan, Romano, Cream Cheese, Mozzarella, Cottage Cheese & Feta

If you want cheese for one-third the cost that is better tasting than your best store-purchased Romano or Parmesan, then this book is for you. Caleb Warnock, the celebrated self-sufficiency master, teaches you how to make seven different cheeses that are delicious, inexpensive, and, most importantly, fun and easy.

Make Your Own Hard Lotion: A Healing Alternative to Traditional Lotions (coauthored by Amberlee Rynn)

Today's liquid commercial lotions have more toxic chemicals than we want to admit. Homemade liquid lotions have a shelf life of only a couple of weeks. Hard lotion is the solution for those interested in avoiding commercial products or lotions with short shelf lives and who want smooth, soft skin.

Amberlee, the owner of the noted Amberlee's Apothecary and a full-time chemist, and Caleb Warnock, the self-sufficiency expert, have teamed up to provide easy-to-make hard lotion solutions for your skin needs by drawing on chemistry and key health ingredients like coconut and avocado oils. Hard lotions are simply the best solution to get the skin you want. And creating your lotion at home is fun and far less expensive than the commercial alternatives.

Hand-Dipped: The Art of Creating Chocolates and Confections at Home (coauthored by Julie Peterson)

Armed with tips on melting, dipping, and molding as well as dozens of rich recipes, you'll be sure to satisfy any sweet tooth. *Hand-Dipped* gives step-by-step instructions that will give amateurs and aspiring professionals alike a deeper look into the process of confection making. Indulge your taste buds with luxurious, easy recipes from *Hand-Dipped*!

ABOUT FAMILIUS

Welcome to a place where mothers and fathers are celebrated, not belittled. Where values are at the core of happy family life. Where boo-boos are still kissed, cake beaters are still licked, and mistakes are still okay. Welcome to a place where books—and family—are beautiful. Familius: a book publisher dedicated to helping families be happy.

VISIT OUR WEBSITE: WWW.FAMILIUS.COM

Our website is a different kind of place. Get inspired, read articles, discover books, watch videos, connect with our family experts, download books and apps and audiobooks, and along the way, discover how values and happy family life go together.

JOIN OUR FAMILY

There are lots of ways to connect with us! Subscribe to our newsletters at www.familius.com to receive uplifting daily inspiration, essays from our Pater Familius, a free ebook every month, and the first word on special discounts and Familius news.

BECOME AN EXPERT

Familius authors and other established writers interested in helping families be happy are invited to join our family and contribute online content. If you have something important to say on the family, join our expert community by applying at:

www.familius.com/apply-to-become-a-familius-expert

GET BULK DISCOUNTS

If you feel a few friends and family might benefit from what you've read, let us know and we'll be happy to provide you with quantity discounts. Simply email us at specialorders@familius.com.

Website: www.familius.com
Facebook: www.facebook.com/paterfamilius
Twitter: @familiustalk, @paterfamilius1
Pinterest: www.pinterest.com/familius

THE MOST IMPORTANT WORK YOU EVER DO WILL
BE WITHIN THE WALLS OF YOUR OWN HOME.